Cambridge Elements

Elements in Contentious Politics
edited by
David S. Meyer
University of California, Irvine
Suzanne Staggenborg
University of Pittsburgh

AGGRIEVED LABOR STRIKES BACK

Inter-sectoral Labor Mobility, Conditionality, and Unrest under IMF Programs

Saliha Metinsoy
Erasmus University Rotterdam

Shaftesbury Road, Cambridge CB2 8EA, United Kingdom

One Liberty Plaza, 20th Floor, New York, NY 10006, USA

477 Williamstown Road, Port Melbourne, VIC 3207, Australia

314–321, 3rd Floor, Plot 3, Splendor Forum, Jasola District Centre, New Delhi – 110025, India

103 Penang Road, #05–06/07, Visioncrest Commercial, Singapore 238467

Cambridge University Press is part of Cambridge University Press & Assessment, a department of the University of Cambridge.

We share the University's mission to contribute to society through the pursuit of education, learning and research at the highest international levels of excellence.

www.cambridge.org
Information on this title: www.cambridge.org/9781009455763

DOI: 10.1017/9781009455749

When citing this work, please include a reference to the DOI 10.1017/9781009455749

First published 2024

A catalogue record for this publication is available from the British Library.

ISBN 978-1-009-45576-3 Hardback
ISBN 978-1-009-45578-7 Paperback
ISSN 2633-3570 (online)
ISSN 2633-3562 (print)

Aggrieved Labor Strikes Back

Inter-sectoral Labor Mobility, Conditionality, and Unrest under IMF Programs

Elements in Contentious Politics

DOI: 10.1017/9781009455749
First published online: April 2024

Saliha Metinsoy
Erasmus University Rotterdam

Author for correspondence: Saliha Metinsoy, metinsoy@essb.eur.nl

Abstract: Why do we see large-scale labor protests and strikes under some IMF programs, such as in Greece in 2010, and not in others, such as in Ireland in the same year? This Element argues that extensive labor market reform conditions in an immobile labor market generate strong opposition to programs. Labor market reform conditions that decentralize and open up an immobile labor market cause workers either to lose in terms of rights and benefits while being stuck in the same job, or to fall into a less protected sector with fewer benefits. Conversely, in more mobile labor markets, wage and benefit differentials are low, and movement across sectors is easier. In such markets, labor groups do not mobilize to the same extent to block programs. I test this theory in a global sample and explore the causal mechanism in four case studies on Greece, Ireland, Latvia, and Portugal.

This Element also has a video abstract: www.cambridge.org/Metinsoy

Keywords: unrest, IMF, labor protests, conditionality, strikes

ISBNs: 9781009455763 (HB), 9781009455787 (PB), 9781009455749 (OC)
ISSNs: 2633-3570 (online), 2633-3562 (print)

Contents

> Since there is imperfect mobility of labor, and wages do not tend to an exact equality of net advantage in different occupations, any individual or group of individuals, who consent to a reduction of money-wages relatively to others, will suffer a relative reduction, which is a sufficient justification for them to resist it.
>
> John Maynard Keynes, 1936

1 Introduction

The International Monetary Fund's (IMF) lending programs are highly controversial and frequently meet violent and nonviolent public responses in borrowing countries. In some countries, we observe a particularly strong labor reaction to IMF programs. Labor groups mobilize to stage protests and strikes to block the programs. Greece in 2010 is one such example, where labor groups organized to protest program measures. However, these reactions are not universal; there is variation across programs. In other cases, we see the implementation of the program without such strong labor opposition or collective mobilizations. In the same year, on the other side of the European Union, Ireland implemented its IMF program without much labor unrest. What explains this variation in labor unrest under IMF programs? Why do we see labor unrest in some cases and not in others?

This Element argues that the IMF's labor market reforms in immobile labor markets generate large-scale grievances and opposition. The IMF's labor market reforms are geared toward bringing greater flexibility and decentralizing labor markets to foster efficient reallocation of workers and promote greater economic productivity (Blanchard et al., 2014, p. 19). To this end, its measures often make hiring and firing easier; decentralize collective bargaining institutions; reduce the minimum wage (in some cases); and ease the restrictive conditions on temporary and part-time employment in labor law. In immobile labor markets, this translates either into immediate job loss for immobile workers – due to the reduced costs of firing – and the prospect of long-term unemployment, or less job security and fewer benefits while staying in the same job. Moving to a new job or sector is discouragingly hard for workers in immobile labor markets as there are extensive wage differentials or differentiated benefits (Hiscox, 2001, p. 9). In such immobile markets, labor groups mobilize to block the implementation of a program that would put them at a distinct disadvantage. In mobile labor markets, on the other hand, wage and benefit differentials (and hence risks) are lower, and movement is easier. Moreover, decreases in income and benefits are less when workers do move to a different sector and periods of unemployment are likely to be shorter. They therefore have less reaction to the programs and we do not observe as much labor unrest in such cases.

I test this theory using a mixed methodology. First, I explore the broad association between labor market mobility, the IMF's labor market reform conditions,[1] and unrest in a global sample of countries between the years 1992 and 2014. I look at the interactive impact of labor market reform conditions and labor (im)mobility on labor unrest using two novel datasets on intersectoral labor mobility and labor unrest as well as checking the robustness of results with established strike and protest datasets in the field. I also investigate the impact of labor immobility at an individual level in terms of prolonged periods of unemployment and economic hardship during an economic crisis using the European Social Survey (ESS) data from Round 5 conducted in European countries between 2010 and 2012, at the height of the Great Recession. Exploring the micro-foundations of unrest, and using the European sample, I show how risk perceptions and economic hardship at the individual level can translate into collective grievances. The quantitative analysis demonstrates the rise in economic grievances due to immobility and the increased likelihood of unrest, all else being equal.

Complementing the quantitative analysis, I demonstrate the adjustment and responsiveness of mobile and immobile labor markets to labor market reform conditions in four European borrowers of the Fund with different levels of labor mobility and labor market reform conditions: Greece (expansive labor market reform conditions and extremely low labor mobility); Ireland (moderate to high levels of labor mobility and no labor market reform under its IMF program); Latvia (high levels of labor mobility and expansive reform conditions); and Portugal (a limited number of labor market reform conditions and moderate to low levels of labor mobility). In Section 5, I also discuss the preexisting institutional setup as a catalyst for unrest and how it (dis)empowers different groups and ideas. I identify two broad political economies. First, in liberal political economies such as Ireland and Latvia, labor market regulation was largely left to the market before the IMF program, labor groups are less cohesive, mobility is high, and the potential for unrest is low. Trade unions find it harder to organize a collective reaction to programs. Second, in dualized labor markets, a group of "insiders" enjoy employment and wage protection with higher pay, while "outsiders" are in precarious jobs with lower pay. In these political economies, the IMF is more forceful in opening up the labor market and reactions are greater not only because mobility is low but also because mobility might mean falling into a less desirable "outsider" category in the labor

[1] Throughout the Element, I use the term "reform conditions" to refer to the conditions attached by the IMF to its loans. The Fund ties its credit to the fulfillment of the policy changes specified in its structural adjustment programs, which are commonly referred to as "conditionality" or "conditions" (Walton and Ragin, 1990, p. 880).

market. Unions are stronger as representatives of "insiders" and have a greater organizational capacity to rally worker groups and organize strikes and protests. In Section 5, I rely on national statistics, interview data with elites such as former ministers, trade union representatives, IMF officials, and European Commission officials as well as selected leadership speeches and documentary analysis.

The Element proposes a novel theory of intersectoral mobility in relation to collective labor mobilizations under IMF programs. Previously, scholars such as John Maynard Keynes (1936) discussed labor mobility with respect to wages, while Henry Bienen and Mark Gersovitz (1985), Michael Hiscox (2001, 2002), and Ronald Rogowski (1989) demonstrated the importance of factor mobility in the manufacturing industry in determining support for trade and political stability. Furthermore, we know that IMF programs have a potent impact on labor groups' income and rights, as discussed by Rodwan Abouharb and David Cingranelli (2007, 2009), Teri Caraway (2006), Gopal Garuda (2000), Manuel Pastor (1987), and James Vreeland (2002). This study expands the theory of factor mobility to intersectoral labor mobility and theorizes the role of intersectoral mobility in relation to labor market reforms and labor unrest under IMF programs. It explains the variation in unrest under IMF programs.

The Element also proposes a comprehensive theory of (im)mobility in the study of contentious politics. As wage earners are almost always the biggest group in society, labor mobility – the easiness of changing jobs and sectors – has important implications for household income, perceptions of risks, spells of unemployment, and ultimately for political choices. If a sector should face an asymmetric shock, especially during an economic crisis, the ability to move to a different job and sector without extensive wage or rights differentials provides individuals with additional security, akin to the safety net afforded by social policies. Policymakers often discuss job mobility as a tool for efficiency in the economy, faster adjustment, and concomitant growth (Zimmermann, 2005). Nevertheless, mobility also has important political implications from a contentious politics perspective. Scholars have previously shown that protests and strikes rise under IMF programs due to increased economic hardship and perceptions of relative deprivation (Pion-Berlin, 1983; Franklin, 1997; Abouharb and Cingranelli, 2007; Reinsberg et al., 2022). This Element disentangles economic hardship under IMF programs and explains that it may not increase for all groups to the same extent. It discusses how hardship might be unequally distributed between mobile and immobile labor groups.

The topic of unrest under IMF programs also has important policy implications for Fund officials, borrowing governments, and labor groups as well as for the future of globalization in general. The IMF's labor market reform conditions in immobile markets increase the human cost of crises, with significant economic and psychological implications for labor groups. Prolonged periods of unemployment and a decline in human capital also take a toll on economic productivity. Moreover, governments often go to the IMF because they cannot find credit on favorable terms in the market (Copelovitch, 2010, p. 3). Labor unrest might further harm market confidence in governments, prolong the programs, and delay the repayment of loans – an outcome that is not desirable either for the Fund or the borrowing government (Appendix III, Interviews No. 4 and No. 7; Woods, 2006, p. 24; Chapman et al., 2017, p. 329). In the interests of labor groups, borrowing governments, and the Fund, program designs could pay closer attention to labor market organization and mobility levels and assign loan conditions in accordance with preexisting industrial relations. Section 6, the Conclusion, discusses potential policy advice in more detail in line with the findings of this Element.

The rest of the Element is organized as follows. Section 2 discusses existing explanations in the literature on unrest under IMF programs and highlights gaps in the literature. It also outlines how this Element contributes to scholarly work on labor mobility and contentious politics. Section 3 explains the underlying theory of labor mobility and the impact of labor market reform conditions in an immobile market as well as the institutional complementarities and how unrest unfolds in different institutional contexts with different (dis)empowered actors. Section 4 tests the impact of labor mobility and labor market reform conditions in a global sample and reports the country- and individual-level evidence. Section 5 discusses four cases with different levels of labor mobility and labor market–related loan conditions as well as different institutional settings – namely, Greece, Ireland, Latvia, and Portugal – in a comparative perspective after the 2008 financial crisis. Section 6 summarizes the argument and findings and discusses some policy implications and further study based on the conclusions of this Element.

2 Unrest under IMF Programs: Existing Explanations

The IMF lends to countries undergoing an economic crisis and that cannot find credit in private markets (they are regarded as too risky by private lenders and interest rates for their government bonds are unsustainably high). The Fund then attaches policy prescriptions to its loans, that is, conditions to be fulfilled by borrowing governments in exchange for its credit. These policy prescriptions and their consequences have been subject to intense scholarly attention.

There is a rich literature on the scope and politics of IMF conditions (Vreeland, 2002; Gould, 2003; Chwieroth, 2007, 2015; Dreher and Jensen,

2007; Steinwand and Stone, 2008; Stone, 2008; Copelovitch, 2010; Nelson, 2014; Dreher et al., 2015; Kentikelenis et al., 2016; Dang and Stone, 2021; Metinsoy, 2022), on the impact of programs on domestic groups and politics (Pastor, 1987; Sidell, 1988; Walton and Ragin, 1990; Nooruddin and Simmons, 2006; Abouharb and Cingranelli, 2007, 2009; Hartzell et al., 2010; Gartzke and Naoi, 2011; Dreher and Gassebner, 2012; Kentikelenis et al., 2016; Casper, 2017; Reinsberg et al., 2019, 2023; Rickard and Caraway, 2019), and on international and domestic outcomes more broadly (Doyle, 2010; Chwieroth, 2014; Chapman et al., 2017; Nelson and Wallace, 2017). However, a study on labor unrest with a specific focus on labor-related issues has yet to be conducted.

The impact of IMF programs on unrest has previously been discussed in the literature, mostly in the context of human rights violations. Rodwan Abouharb and David Cingranelli (2009) look at human rights violations under and outside of IMF programs and find strong evidence that the use of torture and extrajudicial killings increase under the programs. Similarly, David Pion-Berlin (1983) and James Franklin (1997) argue that violent repression increases under IMF programs, since governments have a stake in implementing the programs in order to secure loans from the Fund, repressing the opposition in the process. Although highly plausible and empirically supported, this theory assumes that there will be automatic labor opposition to programs in every country that borrows from the Fund and takes labor opposition for granted. The theory can be further elaborated by analyzing labor protests and strikes in addition to the cases of violent repression. Further elaboration would clarify the causal mechanism of labor opposition to programs rather than considering it an automatic reaction. Scholars such as John Walton and Charles Ragin (1990) show that poverty, especially in contexts of overurbanization, is significantly associated with protests against structural adjustment programs in developing countries. This Element complements their work, first, by discussing another dimension of economic hardship that falls more harshly on immobile groups compared to mobile labor groups and adds further nuance. Second, by delving deeper into the specifics of IMF conditionality and the close relationship between subcategories of the IMF's loan conditions and rising labor opposition in a country, we can explain cross-country variation under IMF programs, such as between Greece and Ireland in 2010 under their respective IMF programs. Finally, this Element complements existing work on protests and strikes that has largely looked at the rise of contentious action under and outside IMF programs.

The literature provides strong evidence that IMF programs can affect domestic politics and political groups, such as exacerbating ethnic and/or political divisions and sowing the seeds of civil war (Hartzell, Hoddie, and Bauer, 2010), precipitating coup d'états (Casper, 2017), fueling governmental instability and crisis (Dreher and Gassebner, 2012), exacerbating inequality and poverty (Oberdabernig, 2013; Lang, 2021), stalling economic growth (Przeworski and Vreeland, 2000; Bas and Stone, 2014), and worsening health services provision and health outcomes (Kentikelenis et al., 2016). The programs can also create an "alienation" effect that triggers civil conflict and protests (Reinsberg et al., 2022).

Manuel Pastor (1987), Gopal Garuda (2000), and James Vreeland (2002), in particular, demonstrate that IMF programs distribute income away from labor groups toward the owners of capital. They show that there is a material basis to labor's discontent beyond the relative deprivation and perceptions that have been referenced to explain labor opposition to programs in previous studies.[2] Teri Caraway (2006) and Bernhard Reinsberg and colleagues (2019) show that labor rights can take a hit under IMF programs. This Element builds on those studies and further specifies the underlying reasons for labor's material disadvantage under programs, the rise of risks and uncertainties in addition to material hardship, and explains the cross-country variation in labor unrest. It contributes to the existing literature by specifically investigating the causes of labor opposition and unrest through underlining "risk" and "uncertainty" and hence the prospective component of material hardship.

In the literature, scholars have also looked at how domestic politics might shape IMF conditions. In particular, Teri Caraway and colleagues (2012) argue that in domestic politics potential labor power can affect labor conditions: namely, that democracies with strong labor groups can avoid intrusive labor conditions. Similar to earlier studies, these authors implicitly assume that labor will always mobilize to oppose such labor conditions. However, they diverge from the earlier studies in emphasizing the organizational capacity of labor groups to resist labor market reform. Their study can further be specified as looking at why and when labor grievances arise. Logically, labor conditions can trigger reactions from affected labor groups. This Element suggests that those reactions will not be uniform and will largely depend on their interaction with the preexisting organization of the labor market. It proposes a theory of labor mobility as a measure of how flexible labor groups are, and how fast they can adapt to the changes brought about by the IMF's labor market–related loan conditions. In cases where groups are largely immobile and the IMF forcefully and suddenly opens up the labor market, those groups would react strongly to these transformative measures.

[2] On relative deprivation theory, see Gurr (2015). For an excellent summary, see Abouharb and Cingranelli (2009, p. 52).

Stroup and Zissimos (2013) argue that, in general, unrest rises under IMF programs due to the unavailability of public employment with structural adjustment programs. They argue that a country's elite cannot use public employment as a way of diffusing discontent and preventing unrest under IMF programs. Scholars have shown that governments can use public employment as a mechanism of compensation (Nooruddin and Rudra, 2014, p. 604) and social insurance (Rodrik, 1998) and that it is a powerful patronage tool (Rickard and Caraway, 2019, p. 5). Under IMF programs, however, this is often not possible either due to budgetary cuts or specific conditions that target the public sector wage bill (Rickard and Caraway, 2019).

Following this line of argument, we can propose that in addition to public employment, mobility functions as a tool of efficient and fast allocation of workers into jobs and sectors that are less affected by an economic crisis and/or austerity measures. In this sense, labor mobility (although it has not yet been extensively discussed in the literature) might be a broader and more generalized diffuser of social discontent than public employment (often a small part of total employment in the job market). In particular, Bienen and Gersovitz (1985), who look at the role of factor mobility in determining the impact of IMF programs on different socioeconomic groups, brilliantly argue that:

> The mobility of factors of production among sectors will be as important in other sectors as it is in government employment. When agricultural prices go down, the returns to land ownership will certainly be depressed, since fertile land is unlikely to have many alternative uses. Agricultural labor may, however, be able to move into an alternative employment, for instance migrating to cities, thereby lessening the impact of a price decrease on labor's welfare. (pp. 741–742)

Bienen and Gersovitz (1985) mainly look at the role of factor mobility across land, labor, and capital. This Element broadens the focus to employment in different sectors in an economy and hence analyzes the mitigating role of smooth movement on labor's welfare in a broader sense. It also specifically looks at labor market–related loan conditions in IMF programs rather than the general impact of structural adjustment.

Varieties of Capitalism scholars discuss labor mobility in different institutional setups (Hall and Soskice, 2001; Hall and Thelen, 2008; Hall and Gingerich, 2009). They propose that labor mobility is higher in liberal market economies (LMEs) due to decentralized and individualized bargaining, fewer welfare benefits, and weaker trade unions. Firing and hiring are both easier in LMEs. Workers are then incentivized to develop portable skills in the absence of a support network and employment and wage protection that they can rely on

(Estevez-Abe et al., 2001). In coordinated market economies (CMEs), on the other hand, collective bargaining is more developed, employment and wage protections are greater, and trade unions are stronger. In CMEs, workers are incentivized to develop specific skills for their industries and hence are less mobile (Estevez-Abe et al., 2001). Varieties of Capitalism scholars, however, often do not tie their discussion of institutional complementarities and labor mobility to (the potential of) contentious action. They often draw attention to "non-zero-sum" interactions and coordination between employer and employee organizations rather than conflict (Korpi, 2006). Furthermore, although their theorization of labor mobility is plausible, it does not match the empirical evidence: CMEs are not less mobile than LMEs; on the contrary, they are more mobile when the business-cycle impact is considered (Hiscox and Rickard, 2002). This is, perhaps, because the Varieties of Capitalism framework conflates incentives with actual labor mobility within the labor market. This Element identifies a novel measurement and conceptualization of labor mobility that can be transferred outside industrialized countries to developing countries and that looks at the "actual" movements of workers across sectors.

Within the Varieties of Capitalism tradition, Peter Hall and Kathleen Thelen (2008, p. 14) discuss institutional change and explain that institutions provide resources for all groups in the economy and are constantly subject to "experimentation, negotiation and conflict" by them. Thelen (2012, 2014) further details institutional change and suggests that institutions adapt to changes in coalitions and shift in response to the social, political, and market contexts in which they are embedded. What happens, however, when there is an external "shock therapy" or "deregulation by surprise" by a potent external actor – the IMF – requires further attention and theorization. This Element argues that the IMF's loan conditions are primarily motivated by bringing flexibility to the labor market and they can clash with preexisting institutional settings, especially when there is an incongruence between those institutions and the IMF's "template" of acceptable policies.[3]

Contentious politics scholars have long demonstrated that economic grievances can motivate protests and strikes (Franzosi, 1995; Gurr, 2015). Social groups organize to protect their interests and influence policy-making. These scholars have not, however, looked at how labor immobility can compound those grievances and lead to an unequal distribution of economic hardship among labor groups. Furthermore, resource mobilization theories in the field of contentious politics, that is, how the organizational capacity of social groups

[3] For more discussion on the neoliberal ideas that dominate the IMF's loan programs, see Woods (2006), Nelson (2014), Ban and Gallagher (2015), and Chwieroth (2015).

can provide the necessary opportunity and opening for aggrieved groups in the field of contentious politics (Shorter and Tilly, 1974; Tilly, 1978; Walton and Ragin, 1990), can be complemented with the "institutions as resources" perspective of the Varieties of Capitalism framework.

Finally, the international political economy literature is clear that economic reform alters preexisting rights and material benefits and reshapes the interests and preferences of groups (Frieden, 1991), and, hence, affects their political allegiances (Rogowski, 1989). It has the potential to trigger political mobilization to place claims (Tilly, 2003). However, how these coalesce, that is, how IMF-sponsored labor market reform proceeds in different institutional settings and its potential for contentious political action, is yet to be examined.

At the intersection of these scholarly traditions, this Element looks at when and why grievances arise in immobile labor markets and how institutional setup and sudden reform under the influence of the IMF are linked to the rise in contentious political action. The next section explains the theory of labor mobility and the impact of the IMF's labor market conditions in an immobile labor market in more detail.

3 Labor Mobility and Adjustment: Material Loss, Risks, and Unrest under IMF Programs

Labor mobility, that is, the ease of changing jobs and sectors (Hiscox, 2001, p. 2), functions as a quasi-social protection mechanism in the labor market. It ensures that individuals can switch to jobs and sectors that are growing or that are less affected by an economic contraction. For instance, more mobile groups are less threatened by trade liberalization and the influx of foreign goods and are more supportive of open trade policies (Hiscox, 2001, 2002, 2020). They are more likely to switch jobs and sectors if their sector becomes less tenable due to increased competition (Hiscox, 2001, p. 2). Moreover, more mobile groups are less dependent on social security than groups with lower mobility (Iversen and Soskice, 2001), as they rely heavily on mobility (rather than social policies) to avoid labor market risks. In general, in the face of uncertainty and/or increased risks in the labor market, individuals might rely on mobility as a substitute for social policy. Mobility ensures that they can move to a new job with a similar income and without long periods of unemployment. For instance, a financial analyst can move to a consultancy job if the financial sector takes a hit. Similarly, an agriculture worker can move to a low-skilled service job if agricultural product prices fall because of foreign competition. However, someone who is trained as a nurse would either require further training to move to a job with similar benefits or would need to accept a reduction in their earnings or benefits when moving to a different job. If collective bargaining institutions are dismantled and their wages decline, they may stay in the same job with reduced income. If they search for another nursing job, they might stay unemployed for a longer period than a worker in a more mobile sector. Similarly, teachers in publicly funded schools may be less mobile than construction sector workers – who can move to mining, for example, if the construction sector takes a hit – especially if there are big wage and benefits differentials with the private sector.

In the absence of labor mobility, individuals are more exposed to labor market risks. This is especially true when IMF programs decentralize labor markets and reduce employment and wage security. Labor conditions required by the IMF often aim at breaking labor market rigidities and enabling efficient allocation of labor groups (Blanchard et al., 2014, p. 5). The Fund's promarket rationale dictates that supply and demand in the labor market ensures the greatest efficiency and productivity (Woods, 2006; Chwieroth, 2007, 2015; Nelson, 2014, 2017). Fund officials often envisage a trade-off between job and wage security and the efficient allocation of workers (Blanchard and Wolfers, 2000, pp. 12–13; Blanchard et al., 2014, p. 7). Prolabor measures such as minimum wage, collective bargaining, strict firing conditions including compensation for dismissal, and restrictions on temporary and part-time contracts are seen as market rigidities that might set wages higher than market-clearing levels while causing unemployment (Blanchard et al., 2014, p. 17).

The IMF's view on flexibility and efficiency in the labor market largely corresponds to LME types. In LMEs, firing and hiring is easier than in CMEs; job turnover is high while job tenure is low (Hall and Gingerich, 2009). Trade unions are relatively weak; employment and unemployment protection is not strong. Collective bargaining coverage is low; individualized and firm-level bargaining is the norm (Estevez-Abe et al., 2001). Conversely, in CMEs, extensive and subsidized vocational training, strong wage-bargaining institutions, and welfare benefits such as unemployment insurance are more common (Hall and Gingerich, 2009). Trade unions are typically stronger (Hall and Soskice, 2001).

In between these ideal types, there are sector-coordinated political economies (Thelen, 2012). These mix characteristics of liberal and coordinated political economies in separate, parallel-functioning labor markets. On the one hand, some sectors are very well-coordinated with strong employment and wage protection; on the other, there are sectors where such protection is minimal or absent (Piore, 1983; Möller, 2015). In such labor markets, we can assume that mobility is lower due to the dualized character of the labor market, and the switch between sectors is inhibited due to wage and protection differentials.

This distinction in the institutional setup is important to this discussion for three reasons. First, the IMF is expected to attach a larger number of labor market reform conditions to its loans in more coordinated and dualized political economies to bring greater flexibility and efficiency in the labor market compared to LMEs. Labor markets in liberal economies already largely rely on market mechanisms. Second, in coordinated and segmented political economies, workers have greater organizational capacity thanks to stronger unions and more widespread collective bargaining coverage (Western, 2020). Furthermore, we know from the contentious politics literature that the degree to which groups are organized significantly affects their capacity to mobilize and stage strikes, protests, and other forms of collective action (Shorter and Tilly, 1974; Tilly, 1978). We can expect a greater number of protests and strikes in more coordinated and dualized labor markets.

Third, and perhaps most importantly, "deregulation, which proceeds through a direct assault on traditional institutions" (Thelen, 2012, p. 147) under IMF programs upsets preexisting labor market relations in dualized and coordinated political economies. It unleashes an almost explosive wave of grievances when the preexisting institutional setup is built on wage and employment protection and collective wage-setting institutions.

When IMF programs suddenly and sharply open up institutionally more coordinated or dualized labor markets, a large group of immobile workers becomes exposed to sudden losses of income and rights. They often face four potential outcomes with significant implications for their income and security. First, they may stay in their jobs but become more insecure, as firing becomes easier. They are more sensitive to such insecurity, as it might be harder for immobile workers to find positions with similar benefits in the event of job loss. Second, their income might fall, since collective bargaining institutions are decentralized and the minimum wage declines. This leads to an overall decline in income across the labor market. Third, they might lose their job specifically due to the IMF programs, which often envisage fiscal cuts and lead to an overall economic contraction (Przeworski and Vreeland, 2000; Vreeland, 2003). Finally, they might face long periods of unemployment or agree to a job with lower benefits to avoid such an outcome. All these potential outcomes are likely to lead to an outburst of discontent and contentious action against the programs. In other words, when the axe of labor market reforms falls on an immobile labor market it triggers a sudden reaction from labor groups, often in the form of large-scale protests and strikes to block program implementation.

Unrest is in this respect prospective; it intends to prevent the implementation of the measures or to achieve their overturn rather than being retrospective. As we will see in Section 5, the announcement of program measures can be sufficient to trigger unrest before their actual implementation. Labor groups quickly organize following the announcement, as in the case of Greece, with the explicit aim of preventing parliament from voting in favor of the measures. In other words, mobile workers "exit," while immobile ones "voice" objection to the measures.

The agency of the political authority and its ability to respond to these demands, however, is significantly compromised under IMF programs. There is an asymmetrical relationship between the IMF and the borrowing government. This is, first, because the IMF is the "lender of last resort" for governments in economic distress. Governments that are unable to find credit with favorable conditions in private markets often apply to the IMF (Copelovitch, 2010). Second, the Fund ties disbursements to the fulfillment of conditions specified in the programs and monitors their implementation (Stone, 2008). Governments are obliged to comply with loan conditions to secure the pledged credit. George Papaconstantinou, the then–finance minister who negotiated Greece's agreement in 2010, summarizes aptly the asymmetry between the IMF and the borrowing government: "When you have your back against the wall; and the clock is ticking because you need to get the money before a bond matures; otherwise you have to declare bankruptcy if you cannot pay; it is not much you can actually negotiate" (Appendix III, Interview No. 3).

Furthermore, labor immobility and IMF-sponsored labor market reforms are likely to interact due to the institutional complementarities I have documented.[4] Labor market reforms are both more likely and have a larger impact on immobile markets and the subsiding impact of mobility on unrest is lower in the case of a stricter and higher number of labor market reform conditions under IMF programs.

In a mobile and flexible labor market, as opposed to an immobile labor market, wage differentials are low (Hiscox, 2001, pp. 16–17; Hiscox and Rickard, 2002, p. 20). When a worker loses their job, it is not discouragingly hard to find a new one with similar benefits and in a relatively short period. In such a market, labor conditions may not trigger large-scale opposition. For example, we saw such a quick and efficient adjustment in Latvia in 2008 and in Ireland in 2010 under their respective IMF programs. To be sure, mobile workers may still not prefer to change jobs, but grievances do not increase to the same extent that leads them to take collective action.

[4] To be sure, there is not a perfect overlap between mobility and labor conditions. There are countries that have low labor mobility (below average mobility in my sample) but did not receive a high number of reform conditions as well as countries with high mobility, which received a large number of labor market reform conditions – such as Latvia in 2008, discussed in Section 5.

Table 1 Interaction between mobility and labor conditionality

		Labor market mobility	
		High	**Low**
Reform conditions	Expansive	Moderate unrest	High unrest
	Nonexpansive	Low unrest	Moderate unrest

We can therefore summarize the interaction between labor conditions and mobility in terms of unrest, as can be seen in Table 1.

Table 1 shows that when there is a low level of labor mobility and expansive labor conditions are assigned under an IMF program, we see a very high level of labor unrest (such as in Greece in 2010). Large-scale strikes and protests will be triggered. When there are fewer labor market reform conditions and high to moderate labor mobility, on the other hand, we observe minimal to no labor unrest (such as in Ireland in 2010). When there is high labor mobility and a significant number of labor market changes, we can expect to see moderate to no unrest (such as in Latvia in 2008). The same is true when there is low labor mobility but fewer labor market reform conditions (i.e. the axe either spares the labor market or falls more gently, such as in Portugal in 2011). Section 5 discusses each case (and its respective IMF programs) in detail. But, before that, the next section tests this theory in a global sample and depicts the broad association between labor mobility, conditionality, and labor unrest under IMF programs.

4 Quantitative Empirical Evidence

> Am I ready to bet money on my results? The answer is a qualified yes. I am ready to bet money on the overall picture that emerges from the use of combined statistical, historical, survey, and ethnographic evidence.
>
> Roberto Franzosi, 1995

The findings of this study suggest that the interaction between preexisting labor mobility in a borrowing country and the extent of labor conditions assigned by the IMF predicts the degree of unrest under the Fund's programs. Furthermore, it shows that increasing risks and uncertainties along with economic hardship prompt individuals to join in collective action against these programs. This section begins with an empirical analysis of the association between mobility, conditionality, and unrest using a global sample of countries in which IMF programs were implemented during the period 1992–2014. It introduces two novel datasets on labor unrest and labor mobility; describes the selected model, measures of labor conditionality, and the control variables; and presents the findings of the analysis. The section also describes a battery of robustness checks performed using alternative model specifications, measurements, and datasets. Additionally, it provides individual-level evidence from a European survey sample, which confirms that labor immobility increases unemployment episodes, compounds economic hardship, and increases the likelihood of individuals' participation in protests.

4.1 Conceptualization and Measurement of Unrest, Mobility, and Conditionality

4.1.1 Measuring Labor Unrest

I measure labor unrest using three different datasets, each with its own coding choices. I mainly rely on the High-Profile Strikes Dataset (HPSD), developed by Robertson and Teitelbaum (2011), which is the data source on labor strikes that is widely endorsed in the literature. This dataset, which covers the period 1980–2005, contains data extracted from news reports. The authors searched for the terms "labor" and "strike" within the "world publications" section of the Nexis database. The compiled data are available for 1,494 country–year observations for countries under an IMF program for at least five months during a particular year (data on participation in IMF programs was derived from Dreher [2006]). The average number of country-level labor strikes in the HPSD is 0.27, with a standard deviation of 1.14. The highest number of strikes (28) was observed in South Korea in 1987.

In addition to relying on HPSD, I constructed a novel dataset on labor unrest for this study and expanded the HPSD to broaden its coverage and comprehensiveness. In this novel dataset, protests, and strikes were searched in the "all English sources" section in the Nexis database and not just the "world publications" section. The use of this approach not only safeguards against duplication of the HPSD but also supports greater objectivity in terms of coverage. The "world publications" section reports events with significant press coverage at a global level, whereas the "all English sources" section also includes local events. In addition, Robertson and Teitelbaum (2011) used "labor" and "strikes" as combined key words for their search. In the novel unrest dataset presented in this study, the coders used the search terms "strike," "protest," and "riot" in separate searches and scanned news reports to determine whether the event reported was labor-related before coding it under its respective category, as opposed to restricting the search term, a priori, to "labor."[5] "Labor-related"

[5] Three student research assistants independently coded the data using the Nexis database. The author arbitrated where clarifications were needed.

issues referred to protests and strikes that were motivated specifically by labor-related issues, centering, for example, on collective agreements and labor rights, easing of firing conditions, reductions in the minimum wage, extended duration of temporary contracts, privatization, asocial and long hours, and changes in labor law. They did not include, for instance, strikes and protests against cuts in government spending; nor were protests and strikes that were primarily motivated by democratic demands included. If any type of violence was reported, then the event was coded as a "riot." The use of a broader search term reduces the likelihood of an arbitrary exclusion of events from the dataset. This new dataset on unrest covers the period 1992–2014. It includes 1,439 country–year observations and is strongly correlated with the HPSD (42 percent, $p < 0.001$). The highest number of strikes in this dataset was observed in Greece in 2012 (twenty-two strikes), and the highest number of protests was recorded in Argentina in 2002 (eight protests).

To account for collective mobilizations, I sum the number of protests, strikes, and riots in a country during a given year. This also speaks to the concerted aspect of collective action, especially under IMF programs, which are short but powerful interventions – programs usually do not last more than three years. During this period, their presence is highly visible and reactions to the programs often unfold in a concerted fashion. Strikes accompany large protests; large protests have the potential to turn into riots; and riots might trigger strikes from labor groups.

Finally, I check the robustness of the results by relying on one of the most widely used and well-established datasets in the field, namely, the Cross-National Time-Series (CNTS) dataset (Banks, 2008; Reinsberg et al., 2022). Protests, strikes, and riots in this dataset were coded with reference to reports in the *New York Times*. However, the dataset has been criticized for its bias toward reporting internationally significant strikes and protests and/or protests and strikes in capital cities and those that involve some sort of violence (Beissinger et al., 2014, p. 338). Robertson and Teitelbaum (2011) also noted that the dataset overreports some protest events in Latin America while under-reporting protests and strikes in Asia. Perhaps more importantly for the study of labor unrest under IMF programs, not all reported protests and strikes in CNTS may be exactly related to labor issues. Nevertheless, the dataset provides wide global coverage and is still useful in this respect. The observations in the CNTS dataset were correlated with the novel dataset on unrest constructed for this study (36 percent, $p < 0.001$) and with the HPSD data set (16 percent, $p < 0.001$). More data on descriptive statistics are presented in Appendix IV.

The datasets do not exclude non-IMF-related protests and strikes. However, as the case studies will show (Section 5), a lot of the protestors and news articles mentioned IMF programs in reports on strikes or protests. This is because IMF programs are highly visible in borrowing countries. The case studies reveal that IMF programs have powerful impacts, striking a country like an axe and unsettling almost all existing political and economic relations. Consequently, almost all economic protests in that country within the program duration are linked to the IMF program.

4.1.2 Measuring Labor Mobility

To measure labor mobility, I construct a new dataset on intersectoral labor mobility for this study. Following Hiscox (2002) and Hiscox and Rickard (2002), I define labor mobility as the ease of changing jobs and sectors and look at yearly changes across sectors calculated as a ratio of the total labor force. The formula for calculating labor mobility can be exressed as follows:

$$\text{Labor mobility}_{j,j,t} = \frac{\sum |E_{i,j,t} - E_{i,j,t-1}| - \left|\sum E_{j,t} - \sum E_{j,t-1}\right|}{0.5^{*}\left(\sum E_{j,t} + \sum E_{j,t-1}\right)}$$

where E denotes the number of workers employed in a sector in a particular year; i denotes the sector; t denotes a particular year; and j denotes the country. The measure first calculates annual changes in the number of workers in a particular sector, for example, construction, from year t-1 to t. After calculating absolute changes in all the sectors considered in the analysis, I sum those changes (the first part of the formula). This first part of the calculation reveals how much cross-sectoral mobility occurred in the labor market within a particular year. Moving to the second part of the formula, I first calculate the change in the total number of workers over two years (i.e. t and t-1) in the labor market (the total for all sectors). This change in the total number of workers accounts for natural movements in and out of the labor market, such as the retirement of some workers and the entry of new graduates. I subtract this natural movement in the labor market from the total cross-sectoral movement. Finally, I convert the measure into a ratio of the total workforce by dividing it by the average number of workers in the labor market over the two years, as there is naturally a greater movement in and out of the market in larger countries (expressed in the denominator of the formula). This ratio can be interpreted as the percentage of workers that moved across sectors from one year to the next after the natural movement in and out of the market is accounted for (see Appendix I for a full list of the sectors included).

To calculate mobility, I used the ILOSTAT data on "total employment by economic activity" for the period 1992–2021 (ISIC 4).[6] The data in this database are complete for all countries and all years thanks to the projections

[6] The data can be accessed on the ILOSTAT website: https://ilostat.ilo.org/topics/employment/.

of economic activity made by local offices of the International Labour Organization (ILO), therefore there are no missing data.

Changes in labor mobility ranged between 0 percent (indicating very little or no movement) and 15 percent of the labor force (extensive movement) in the dataset, with a mean value of 1.5 percent in the sample of IMF countries available for 1,431 country–year observations. There is a large number of near-zero values for this variable, as mobility across sectors is challenging and hence rare for most workers. This type of intersectoral movement becomes crucial, especially when a sector experiences asymmetric shock and shrinking employment opportunities. To the best of my knowledge, this is the first global dataset on intersectoral labor mobility reported in the literature; it complements and extends Hiscox and Rickard's dataset on mobility within manufacturing sectors in industrialized countries that is based on the OECD STAN database (Hiscox and Rickard, 2002).

Figure 1 shows that mobility had an impact on reducing strike events. On average, fewer strikes occurred when the mobility value rose above the average (1.5 percent).

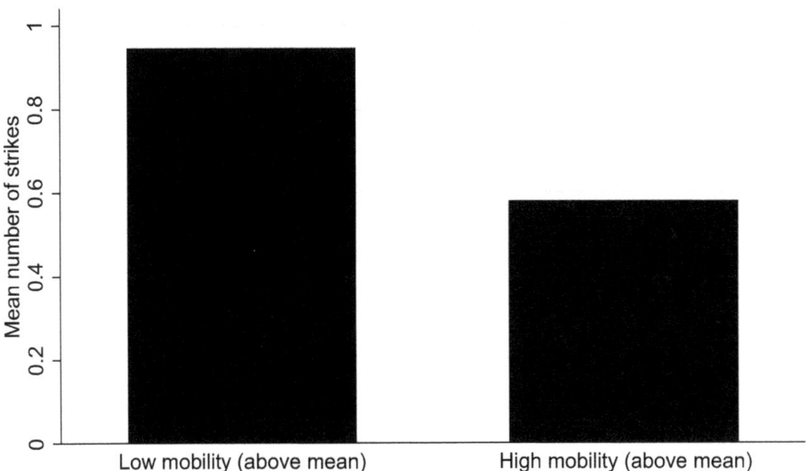

Figure 1 Average number of strikes for low- and high-mobility countries under IMF programs

Source: Data on mobility is based on the author's calculations of mobility using the ILOSTAT dataset; data on strikes came from the HPSD developed by Robertson and Teitelbaum (2011). The results were very similar when the analysis was rerun using the new unrest dataset and the CNTS (2012) dataset.

Mobility also has a slightly reducing impact on anti-government demonstrations recorded in the CNTS dataset, but the impact was less pronounced than that for strikes ($p = 0.08$). The reason may be that striking is the main instrument deployed by workers to express their discontent regarding labor-related matters.

There is considerable variation in mobility across countries, regions, and years. Figure 2 shows average mobility across different regions during the period 1992–2021.

A question that arises is whether mobility is time-variant, as it relates to the long-term organization of the labor market. Indeed, average labor mobility in the full sample fluctuated across the years, as demonstrated in Figure 3. Mobility is fundamentally an adaptation strategy deployed by workers, with labor groups switching sectors when they are able, *and* forced, to do so. For instance, mobility levels in Ireland and Latvia – two highly mobile countries included in this study – fluctuated significantly across the years (see the case studies presented in Section 5).[7] The case studies reveal that there was not only significant variation in average mobility across countries but also within countries. Notably, in countries where there was more mobility, there was a significant increase in sector-switching when an economic crisis occurred (measured as a decline in GDP per capita income relative to the previous year). By contrast, in more rigid, less mobile markets, mobility levels decreased during crisis periods, presumably because workers held on to their jobs when the economic growth declined.

The significant variation in intersectoral mobility across years also shows that cross-sectoral mobility is a better measure of mobility compared with commonly used measures reported in the literature – for instance, employment protection legislation (EPL) (see, e.g., Estevez-Abe et al., 2001). Employment protection legislation does not show significant variation, as labor laws are not

[7] This discussion raises an important question regarding the origins of this mobility. Economists who have extensively studied the phenomenon at an individual level have found that white-collar workers are less mobile than blue-collar workers, which partly explains why some developing countries exhibited higher levels of mobility than developed countries in the sample. However, the reasons why wage differentials increase and protection across sectors differs also merit a political–economic analysis. Although such an investigation is beyond the scope of this Element, one can speculate that in countries where there are big differences in incomes and rights between the formal sector, where "insiders" are strongly protected, and the informal sector, where no protection exists (as in Greece), the labor market would be highly immobile. In countries where there is strict government regulation to maintain a certain evenness of protection relating to baseline wages and rights across sectors, higher levels of mobility may be apparent. However, future studies should inquire into the political reasons for this economic outcome, notably high wage differentials across sectors. In particular, clear and consistent regulation, progressive income taxation, and social policies may play important roles in maintaining a level playing field across economic sectors.

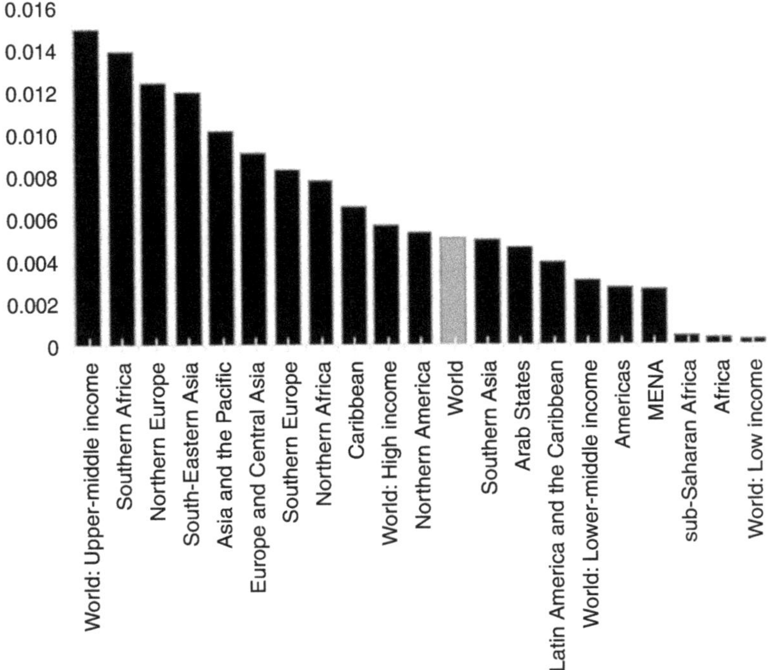

Figure 2 Average labor mobility across regions, 1992–2021

Source: Author's own calculations based on ILOSTAT data.

Note: The y-axis shows intersectoral mobility as a ratio of the total workforce.

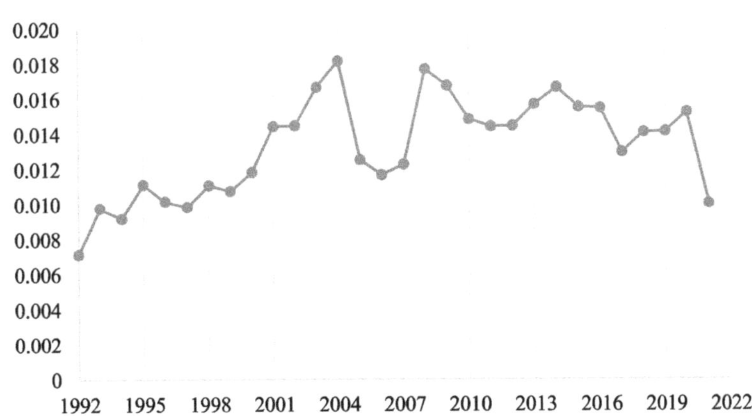

Figure 3 Average labor mobility across years (global sample), 1992–2021

Source: Author's own calculations based on ILOSTAT employment data.

Note: The y-axis indicates intersectoral mobility as a ratio of the total workforce.

easily changed. Furthermore, EPL could be conflating incentives to move with *actual* movement when the need arises – for example, when a sector is impacted by an asymmetrical shock (Hiscox and Rickard, 2002). Another common measure of mobility reported in the literature is job tenure. However, unlike the measure of cross-sectoral mobility used in this study, job tenure does not capture movement across sectors. Job turnover could be high because of frequent unemployment episodes, for example. Cross-sectoral mobility may be a better measure of the absorption capacity of different sectors during hard times. As Section 5 will show, in the Latvian case, for instance, during a period of decline in economic outputs, the number of persons employed in the manufacturing sector increased, while employment in the construction sector significantly declined. Similarly, in Ireland, employment in the service sector declined, whereas employment in the accommodation and food services sectors increased. Conversely, in a more rigid market, such as that of Greece, employment collapsed across all sectors, leading to skyrocketing unemployment.

4.1.3 Measuring Labor Conditionality

To measure labor conditionality, I use the dataset developed by Kentikelenis et al. (2016). This dataset covers wage conditions and employment conditions, such as hiring and firing restrictions, collective agreements, individual- and firm-level wage agreements, pensions, and social security provisions, such as unemployment benefits and the unemployment replacement ratio. It excludes conditions that are beneficial for labor. Consequently, the conditions included in the dataset all entail some sort of disadvantage affecting labor groups.[8] The implementation of these conditions is not included in the analysis, as the specification of a condition in the Letter of Intent would be sufficient for labor groups to mobilize and stage protests and strikes.[9] In other words, labor groups react to the prospect of conditions being implemented that would put them at a distinct disadvantage. A simple count of labor conditions within the sample ranged from 0 (no labor condition) to 13. Descriptive statistics for all variables are shown in Appendix V.

To establish comparability with earlier studies, I also weigh labor conditions in accordance with their stringency (see Caraway et al., 2012, p. 42). In IMF programs, four basic types of conditions are entailed: prior actions, performance

[8] There are several other conditionality datasets in the literature. However, most of these are not publicly available and/or cover shorter periods, including the IMF's own Monitoring of Funds Arrangement (MONA) database. The latter, however, is not very clear, and some entries are randomly missing for unspecified reasons (Kentikelenis et al., 2016).

[9] A Letter of Intent is a program outline written by the borrowing government in cooperation with IMF staff and submitted to the IMF for approval. It specifies the policies the government will implement in exchange of IMF loans.

criteria, structural benchmarks, and indicative benchmarks. These four types of conditions do not carry equal weight (Caraway et al., 2012, p. 42). Prior actions and performance criteria are stringent: prior actions must be fulfilled before the program starts, while performance criteria are prerequisites for its continuation, with the disbursement of the next tranche being contingent on their fulfillment. They can only be waived by the IMF Board. Following Kentikelenis et al. (2016), I multiplied strict conditions (prior actions and performance criteria) by two. Structural benchmarks and indicative targets are binding conditions. However, their fulfillment is not tied to the disbursement of loans. Therefore, I generated a "weighted labor conditionality" variable summing the simple count of indicative and structural benchmarks and the multiplied count of prior actions and performance criteria. Weighted labor conditions in the sample changed between 0 (no condition) and 26 (strict conditionality) during the period 1989–2014 with a mean value of 1.36 and a standard deviation of 2.84.

Finally, I examine the relative frequency of labor conditions in relation to the total conditions. I divided the number of labor conditions in a particular country during a particular year by the total number of conditions during that year and for that particular country. The measure ranged from 0 (no labor condition) to 0.5 (exactly 50 percent of all conditions within the program were labor conditions). The countries with the highest proportion of labor conditions within their programs (i.e. 50 percent) were Belarus in 2008, Estonia in 1999, Hungary in 1989, and Uruguay in 2007.

Figure 4 shows that the relative frequency of labor conditions in programs has changed over the years. Whereas it increased gradually up to 2005, it showed a declining trend from 2006. This change can be attributed to the establishment of the Independent Evaluation Office in 2001 and strong criticism of IMF programs during the Asian financial crisis in the late 1990s and early 2000s. The impact of this criticism seems to have somewhat sluggishly led to an actual reduction in labor conditions within IMF programs. To control for this potential IMF-induced impact, I add year-fixed effects along with country-fixed effects to control for any unaccounted country-level impacts.

Labor conditions and mobility seem to interact as predicted by the theory. A substantive and statistically significant negative relationship exists between mobility and all three measures of labor conditions within the programs.[10]

[10] The negative relationship between labor conditions and mobility is logical, as more rigid, immobile markets would be expected to have more labor conditions. A senior IMF official suggested: "We [IMF staff] follow the principle of 'parsimonious conditions' that are critical to the success of the program. That is, conditionality is assigned only in areas where there is a 'problem.' Unless there is a labor market problem, no labor conditions would be assigned" Rigid markets where there is limited reallocation are viewed as problematic by the IMF (Blanchard et al., 2014).

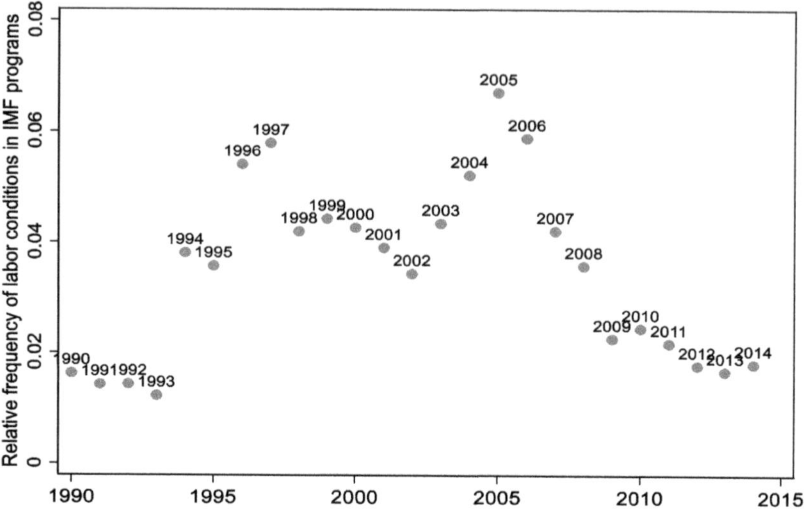

Figure 4 Relative frequency of labor conditions in IMF programs, 1990–2014
Source: IMF conditionality dataset (Kentikelenis et al., 2016).

Indeed, an increase in the mobility score by 1 percentage point reduces the share of labor conditions by 19 percent.[11] The negative relationship between labor conditions and mobility is expected by the theory; we indeed expect to see more labor conditions in more rigid, immobile markets. There is accumulating evidence in the literature that the IMF might indeed assign labor conditions based on political concerns rather than with an economic rationale. Caraway et al. (2012) show that strong labor groups, for instance, might avoid labor conditions. Similarly, Metinsoy (2022) shows that US-allied left-wing governments receive more labor conditions, signaling their ideological proximity to the United States. To safeguard against potential endogeneity, I instrument for labor conditions and IMF program participation in the statistical model. The next section presents the model specifications in more detail.

4.2 Model Specifications

An empirical analysis of the impacts of IMF programs on unrest is not straightforward because of issues relating to sample selection (Vreeland, 2003; Stone, 2008; Stubbs et al., 2020). One could argue that systematic commonalities among IMF borrowers, such as poverty or an acute economic crisis, can cause unrest and not IMF programs or the conditionality attached to programs per se

[11] This calculation is based on an OLS regression analysis conducted for panel data with fixed effects when the sample was restricted to countries under an IMF program during a particular year. When an outlier of 0.5 was excluded from the relative frequency of labor conditions, the association dropped to 17 percent.

(Przeworski and Vreeland, 2000, p. 387; Steinwand and Stone, 2008, pp. 125 and 602). Furthermore, similar factors that result in countries becoming the recipients of more labor conditions may be associated with rising unrest. For instance, democracies could provide greater opportunities for collective mobilization, and they may be more likely to sign up for an IMF program and opt for labor conditions to initiate labor market reforms while bypassing domestic political opposition. To address this problem, following Stubbs et al. (2020) I fit a "three simultaneous equations" model with compound instruments that address selection into IMF programs and into labor conditions, and analyze the impacts of mobility and conditionality on labor unrest within three interconnected simultaneous equations. The model fits a maximum likelihood estimate (MLE).

The first equation addresses selection into IMF programs. Here, the IMF participation variable is coded 1 if a country had an IMF program for at least five months in a specific year; otherwise, it is coded 0. Data came from Dreher, Sturm, and Vreeland (2015). Following a recent innovation in the literature, I instrumentalize IMF program participation via the interaction between a country's average program participation during the study period (1980–2014) and the IMF's budgetary constraint (Nelson and Wallace, 2017; Stubbs et al., 2020; Lang, 2021). The IMF's budgetary constraint is measured by the ratio of the Fund's liquid resources, such as Special Drawing Rights (SDR) contributions and the usable sum of currencies. Liabilities are outstanding payments to borrowers (i.e. its upcoming lending arrangements) and the resources that the Fund has borrowed from its members (i.e. the Fund's debt) (Nelson and Wallace, 2017; Stubbs et al., 2020; Lang, 2021). Data on the IMF's budgetary constraint came from Lang (2021). As Lang (2021) has explained, countries with a history of borrowing from the Fund are much more likely to be prioritized when the IMF's budget is constrained. When the Fund has greater resources, its lending is more liberal. This measure, that is, the interaction between the IMF's liquidity and average past program participation, has a very strong predictive power for IMF program participation (Nelson and Wallace, 2017; Stubbs et al., 2020; Lang, 2021). Furthermore, the instrument fulfills the exclusion criterion. As proposed in the literature, the interaction of an endogenous variable (IMF program participation) with an exogenous variable (IMF's budgetary constraint) could be interpreted as being exogenous. It follows from the fact that the amount that the IMF lends in a particular year, and hence how far its resources are stretched, is independent of any one borrower's domestic political and economic processes and outcomes (Lang, 2021). Following earlier studies, I took the natural logarithm of the IMF liquidity variable to overcome skewness and generated an interaction term entailing average IMF program participation and the natural logarithm of the liquidity measure. The model fits a probit model for the binary IMF selection variable.

To predict labor conditions, following Stubbs et al. (2020) I again use the instrument of the interaction between the average number of labor conditions for a country over the period of analysis and the IMF's budgetary constraint. The use of this instrument was based on the argument that endogenous processes are likely to result in similar lines of conditionality in repeat borrowers. Furthermore, the number of conditions would be expected to decrease when there is less demand on the Fund's resources (and hence increased liquidity). Conversely, the stringency and the number of conditions are expected to increase when the Fund's resources are diminished (and liquidity decreases) (Dreher and Vaubel, 2004; Stubbs et al., 2020). This is because the IMF would be cautious about the use of its resources and apply more stringent controls (Dreher and Vaubel, 2004). Once again, the interaction of an endogenous variable with an exogenous one would yield exogenous results under mild assumptions (for further discussion, see Stubbs et al., 2020). The instrument of labor conditions is particularly appropriate for addressing potential endogeneity between labor conditions and unrest via the strength of labor groups in this study. If a country has strong labor groups they could have an influential role in organizing collective action, such as strikes and riots, as well as in reducing labor conditions by threatening collective action (Caraway, Rickard, and Anner, 2012), potentially causing unrest and labor conditions to become endogenous. This concern was addressed by using an instrumental variable for labor market reform conditions. The Fund's liquidity (i.e. its available resources) is not linked to the strength of labor groups in a borrowing country. In other words, how much the IMF lends to its other member countries, and when, is unlikely to be associated with the power of labor groups in that particular country. The model fits a quasi-linear equation for the labor conditions variable.

The third and final equation includes labor strike events as the dependent variable, which was derived from the HPSD. I added 1 to the *event* variable and took the natural logarithm of the variable to remove skewness – another common practice in the field for count data with typically large numbers of zeros (see, for instance, Reinsberg et al., 2022). For robustness checks, I follow the same procedure using the following variables: "strikes," "riots," and "anti-government demonstrations" derived from the CNTS dataset (2015), as well as the unrest dataset coded for this study.

4.3 Control Variables

A "three simultaneous equations" model means that I control for several variables that can affect selection into IMF programs, conditionality, and unrest. These variables are *GDP per capita income* (the frequency of strikes and protests is higher in richer countries, whereas poorer countries are more likely to borrow from the Fund); *GDP per capita growth* (crisis prompts more protests and strikes as well as increasing the likelihood of an IMF program); and *total population* (more populated countries have higher frequencies of strikes and protests and are also more likely to sign up for an IMF program) (Fearon and Laitin, 2003, p. 81). Data for all three variables came from the World Bank's World Development Indicators (WDIs). I lag GDP per capita income and per capita growth by one year to exclude the potential impact of the IMF program and adopt the natural logarithm of the population variable to remove skewness.

I also control for *democratic governments* in the analysis, as democratic countries provide more opportunities for political participation in activities such as strikes and protests and are less likely to engage in their violent repression compared with nondemocratic regimes (Hegre, 2001; Dahl, 2020). Furthermore, democracies are more likely to borrow from the IMF (Stone, 2008). Data for the democracy variable came from the Polity II dataset, with 0 indicating the most authoritarian regimes and 20 indicating the most democratic ones.[12]

Lastly, where the *urban population* accounts for a comparatively high proportion of the total population this is likely to be associated with an increased frequency of strikes and unrest-related actions, as opportunities for collective mobilization are greater in cities compared with rural areas. Furthermore, overurbanization is shown to be related to the rise of protests and strikes under structural adjustment programs (Walton and Ragin, 1990). Data for the proportion of the population living in urban areas came from the HPSD.

4.4 Empirical Results

Table 2 presents the empirical results of the compound instrumental variable analysis.

Table 2 shows that the interaction term is statistically and substantively significant for predicting strike events after a country's selection into the IMF program and selection into labor conditions are accounted for. As expected, mobility significantly reduces the number of strikes observed under IMF programs. The marginal impact of mobility, with all other variables held at their mean values, is approximately two strike events. In other words, a percentage

[12] In the original dataset, -10 indicates the most authoritarian governments, and 10 indicates the most democratic ones. I recoded the data using a 20-point scale for ease of interpretation.

Table 2 Analysis of the compound instrumental variables across three simultaneous equations

First equation: Strike events (logged)	
	Coefficient
IMF participation	-0.0758
	(0.227)
Mobility score	-0.418
	(0.711)
Labor conditions	0.00432
	(0.187)
Mobility score x labor conditions	-0.371**
	(0.159)
Democracy	0.00361
	(0.00913)
Urban population (% of the population)	0.0158
	(0.0128)
Lagged GDP per capita	-5.65e–07
	(1.00e–06)
Population (logged)	0.485*
	(0.282)
Lagged GDP per capita growth	1.07e–05
	(1.46e–05)
Constant	-8.754*
	(4.913)
Number of observations	1,691
Country-fixed effects	Yes
Yearly fixed effects	Yes
Second equation: IMF program participation	
Mobility score	5.045
	(10.33)
Labor conditions	0.308
	(5.016)
Democracy	0.0346
	(0.346)
Urban population (% of the population)	-0.00520
	(0.294)
Lagged GDP per capita	-1.06e–05
	(2.16e–05)

Table 2 (cont.)

Population (logged)	-1.198
	(1.431)
Lagged GDP per capita growth	-0.000366
	(0.00111)
Compound IMF participation instrument	-2.505
	(7.067)
Constant	23.31
	(0)
Number of observations	1,691
Country-fixed effects	Yes
Yearly fixed effects	Yes
Third equation: Labor conditionality	
Mobility score	-1.012
	(1.908)
Democracy	0.0413
	(0.0262)
Urban population (% of the population)	-0.0298
	(0.0356)
Lagged GDP per capita	2.69e–06
	(2.17e–06)
Population (logged)	-0.809
	(1.801)
Lagged GDP per capita growth	-5.61e–05**
	(2.27e–05)
Compound labor conditions instrument	-0.273
	(2.160)
Constant	14.76
	(29.77)
Number of observations	1,691
Country-fixed effects	Yes
Yearly fixed effects	Yes

Notes: Robust standard errors are in parentheses. ***$p < 0.01$, **$p < 0.05$, *$p < 0.1$.

point increase in mobility reduces the count of strike actions by two. This finding is highly significant as the range of strike events in the dataset is twenty-eight. Furthermore, the decreasing impact of mobility changes, depending on the level of labor conditions. Figure 5 depicts this differentiated impact.

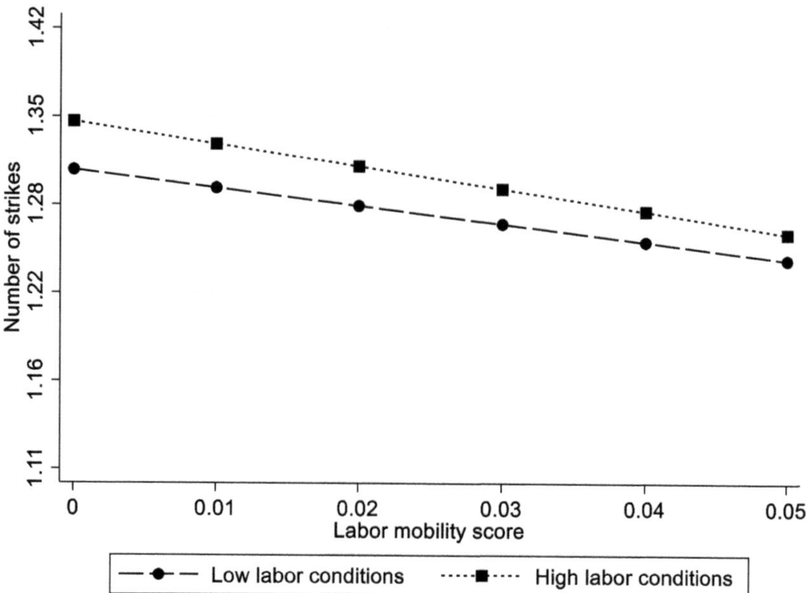

Figure 5 Predicted number of strikes at different levels of mobility and labor conditionality

Source: Labor conditionality dataset (Kentikelenis et al., 2016).

Note: The mobility calculations were based on ILOSTAT data. High labor conditions refer to a simple count of five or more labor conditions occurring in a country–year. Low labor conditions refer to fewer than five labor conditions.

Figure 5 shows that when a high number of labor conditions (i.e. more than five) is observed during a country–year, the expected number of strikes was higher at each level of mobility compared with low conditionality (fewer than five conditions). The difference somewhat decreases at higher levels of mobility, indicating that once a certain level of mobility is achieved, an increase in labor conditions does not necessarily trigger strike action to the same extent.

In line with recent standards evidenced in the literature, I do not interpret the impact of control variables, as their impact is conditional on potential confounders. The main goal of this study is to determine the partial impact of the interaction term between mobility and conditionality after accounting for this term's cofounders. All control variables are accordingly specified from this perspective. Potential confounders for variables, such as the democracy variable, were not specified, and the interpretation may not, therefore, reflect the actual impact of this variable (Hünermund and Louw, 2020). Next, I check the robustness of these findings, fitting three different model specifications and using alternative measures for strikes, protests, riots, and industrial disputes.

4.5 Robustness Checks

For robustness checks, I test the impact of the interaction term of mobility and conditionality using three of the most commonly used models described in the literature, while investigating the impact of IMF programs on domestic outcomes. These models are a two-stage selection model for count-dependent variables, an ordinary least square (OLS) used for panel data with fixed effects, and a negative binomial regression for panel data. I also rerun the models using alternative dependent variables.

Two-stage models that account for selection into IMF programs are widely used to study the impact of IMF programs on economic and political outcomes. They start from the observation that there is nonrandom selection into IMF programs, which is likely to affect political outcomes under these programs (Vreeland, 2003, 2007). For example, it could be argued that countries that borrow from the IMF are especially conflict- and unrest-prone. Thus, it is these preexisting vulnerabilities, and not IMF programs per se, that generate unrest. Accordingly, systematic commonalities among IMF borrowers must be accounted for.

However, econometric models that account for selection during the first stage, when the dependent variable in the second stage is a count one, are not very common and are only just developing (Wyszynski and Marra, 2018). The application of these models in panel data analysis is even more rare. Some of the early studies on labor conditions ran a simple negative binomial regression with robust standard errors clustered across countries for panel data. However, this approach does not address the sample selection problem; nor does clustering standard errors across countries adequately account for the properties of panel data.

I run a selection model for count-dependent variables using a newly developed R software package, SemiParSampleSel, which was specifically designed for selection models with count-dependent variables to perform robustness checks and to establish comparability with previous studies (Wyszynski and Marra, 2018). This new model fits a negative binomial regression for the dependent variable using a penalized MLE after accounting for selection into IMF programs in the first stage. It also links a sample selection function to the outcome function, hence fitting a two-stage model. The negative binomial model is particularly appropriate in this study, given its specific focus on nonnormally distributed count data (Cameron and Trivedi, 2013). As labor unrest is not very common, there are many zeros for the dependent variable. The unit of analysis is once again country–year.

Previous studies identified factors that are likely to affect self-selection into IMF programs, such as economic crisis (a reduced GDP per capita growth rate; Stone, 2008, p. 604), an imbalance in the budget, measured as a deteriorating current account balance and increasing external debt expressed as a percentage of gross national income (GNI) (Copelovitch, 2010), and recidivism (previous borrowers are more likely to return to the Fund) (Stone, 2008; Rickard and Caraway, 2014). While investigating self-selection into IMF programs, I look at the impact of those variables following the earlier literature. The dependent variable is IMF program participation, coded 1 if the country was under an IMF program for at least five months in a particular year, and otherwise coded 0. The IMF participation data came from Dreher et al. (2015). Data for economic variables, such as GDP growth, current account balance, and external debt service came from the World Bank's WDI dataset. To measure recidivism, I follow Stubbs et al. (2020) and calculate the average instances of IMF participation in the preceding five years.

In the second part of the analysis, I examine the impact of the interaction between mobility and labor conditionality measured via three different variables: labor condition count, weighted labor conditions, and the relative frequency of labor conditions. The dependent variable is the number of strike events from the HPSD.

The results of the two-stage analysis are shown in Table 3. They confirm some of the findings of the earlier studies on selection into IMF programs. Specifically, they show that an economic recession in a country measured through decline in GDP per capita growth increases the likelihood of signing up to an IMF program. Accumulating external debt similarly increases the probability of a country concluding an IMF agreement. However, contrary to the expectations reported in the literature, countries with a higher GDP and a positive current account balance (as a percentage of GDP) are more likely to apply to the IMF. It appears that compared with other variables, negative growth and rising external debt are more likely to prompt governments to borrow from the IMF. Lastly, recidivist borrowers are not necessarily more likely to return to the IMF to request credit after the economic factors are accounted for.

The second part of the analysis once again shows that the interaction between mobility and conditionality has a negative and statistically significant impact. With higher numbers of labor conditions, the impact of mobility, as an adaptive tool against social risk, becomes more visible. When mobility has a value of zero, labor market reform conditions have an increasing effect on strike events by 0.004. When labor conditions are at zero, mobility too has an increasing impact on strikes. This finding might be capturing some of the impact of IMF programs on inducing strikes.

Table 3 Two-stage model: IMF participation and the impacts of mobility and conditionality

First stage: Selection into IMF programs

Variables	**Self-selection into IMF programs**
GDP per capita growth	-9.491e–04***
	(9.938e–12)
GDP	2.534e–12***
	(7.862e–17)
External debt (% of GNI)	6.835e–15***
	(6.230e–18)
Current account balance (% of GDP)	1.583e–16***
	(4.769e–04)
Recidivism	-7.970e–07
	(2.968e–05)
Constant	4.347e–13
	(1.966e–06)

Second stage: Impacts of mobility and conditionality on strikes

Variables	**Strike event**
Mobility	1.186***
	(1.114e–07)
Labor conditions	3.731e–03***
	(1.278e–10)
Mobility x labor conditions	-0.5658***
	(1.898e–08)
GDP per capita	4.894e–05***
	(2.334e–13)
Population (logged)	0.1882***
	(9.310e–10)
Democracy	0.02539***
	(1.651e–10)
Urban population	7.081e–03***
	(4.932e–11)
Constant	-7.032***
	(1.538e–08)
Number of observations	978

Notes: Probit for panel data in the first stage of the analysis. A negative binomial regression was conducted for the second stage. Robust standard errors are in parentheses. ***$p < 0.001$; **$p < 0.01$, *$p < 0.05$, +$p < 0.1$.

In addition, I check the robustness of the results using an OLS model with robust standard errors clustered across countries and three different dependent variables. These variables are the logged strike event variable, the unrest variable (the sum of all protests, strikes, and riots) derived from the unrest dataset, and the unrest variable derived from the CNTS dataset. I treat unrest variables as quasi-continuous variables, as they ranged in value from 0 to 75 in the unrest dataset and up to 85 in the CNTS dataset. The sample in this model is restricted to countries participating in IMF programs for at least five months in a particular year. Even though restricting the sample to IMF program countries and excluding others results in an underestimation of the impact of the independent variables (because it inflates standard errors), this strategy might still yield more reliable results, as it excludes "false zeros" for labor conditions. Alexander Kentikelenis and colleagues (2016) code labor conditions as 0 for non-IMF program countries as well as for countries that did not receive any labor conditions in a particular year. Obviously, the case of a country that does not receive any labor conditions because it is not under an IMF program differs from that of a country that borrows from the Fund but does not receive any labor conditions. Hence, to exclude 0 values for labor conditions in non-IMF program countries, I restrict the sample to those countries with an IMF program implemented for a minimum of five months during a particular year. Table 4 shows the results of the analysis.

The interactive impact of mobility and labor conditionality on labor unrest remains substantively significant in these models as well. The impact is also statistically significant in the first two models (when the dependent variables are strike events based on the HPSD and the unrest variable based on the new unrest dataset). When both mobility and conditionality have values of 0, the expected count for unrest is an additional 0.27 events. Labor conditions increase the expected number of protests and strikes. When the value of mobility is 0 and there are five additional labor conditions in the program, the count of unrest increases to 0.37 events, all else being equal. When there are ten conditions, the expected unrest count goes up to 0.46. By contrast, mobility reduces expected strikes and protests. When there are five conditions under a program, and the mobility score during that year is 0.04, the expected unrest declines to 0.22.

Finally, I examine the impact of mobility and labor conditionality on labor unrest using a negative binomial regression for panel data for robustness checks, which are the powerhouse models for count variables within the literature. The unit of analysis is again an IMF program. The impact of mobility and conditionality remains substantively and statistically significant in these models as well. Whereas mobility has a decreasing impact on unrest, labor conditionality has an increasing influence. The statistical significance, however, decreases relative to the preferred method of instrumenting for selection into IMF

Table 4 Robustness checks: Ordinary least square (OLS) model

Variables	Strike event	Unrest	CNTS unrest
Mobility score	-0.722	0.781	7.630
	(0.895)	(1.454)	(8.491)
Labor conditions	-0.000513	0.0194	-0.0365
	(0.00594)	(0.0175)	(0.0323)
Mobility score x labor conditions	-0.450***	-0.907**	-1.892
	(0.175)	(0.429)	(1.538)
Democracy	0.00316	0.0186*	0.0115
	(0.00406)	(0.0111)	(0.0414)
Urban population (% of the population)	0.00305	-0.000394	-6.16e−05
	(0.00209)	(0.00421)	(0.00968)
Lagged GDP per capita	7.63e−06	6.40e−05	4.13e−05
	(8.20e−06)	(4.74e−05)	(3.12e−05)
Population (logged)	0.133***	0.187***	0.544***
	(0.0253)	(0.0510)	(0.185)
Lagged GDP per capita growth	1.03e−05	6.25e−05	-3.27e−05
	(2.35e−05)	(4.38e−05)	(6.39e−05)
Constant	-2.177***	-3.358***	-7.826***
	(0.409)	(0.916)	(2.725)
Number of observations	847	847	843
Number of country codes	94	94	94

Notes: OLS for panel data. Robust standard errors are shown in parentheses. ***$p < 0.01$, **$p < 0.05$, *$p < 0.1$.

programs and labor conditionality. A potentially endogenous relationship probably inflates the standard errors. The results for negative binomial models are presented in Appendix V.

In the next section, I provide individual-level evidence derived from the ESS on the role of mobility in reducing economic hardship and the duration of periods of unemployment while also reducing the likelihood of joining protests. Individual-level evidence not only complements the country-level empirical evidence but also demonstrates how mobility functions as a diffuser of social risk within the labor market.

4.6 Individual-Level Analysis: Immobility, Unemployment, and Economic Hardship

The theory proposed in this Element is premised on the fact that labor market immobility prolongs periods of unemployment, which has ramifications for individuals' incomes, increasing their perceptions of risk and uncertainty. Although a global dataset on individuals' mobility levels currently does not exist, the ESS, conducted at the height of the eurozone crisis in 2010, offers a unique opportunity to test some of these claims at the individual level. Round five of the ESS was conducted between 2010 and 2012 in twenty-eight European countries (including non-EU members, notably Russia and Ukraine). That specific round included a mobility-related item which was not subsequently repeated in other waves of the ESS. The survey asked the question: "How difficult or easy would it be for you to get a similar or better job with another employer if you had to leave your current job?" Respondents were asked to assess the level of easiness/difficulty using a 10-point scale, with 10 being *extremely easy* and 0 being *extremely difficult*. It can be posited that individuals with lower scores, who believed that it would be very difficult to move to a job offering similar benefits, were less mobile than those with higher scores, who felt that job changes would be easy. The scale measures the self-assessed mobility of individuals, with one caveat: individuals may have underrated or overrated their mobility. Yet, perceptions of mobility are perhaps equally – if not more – important than the "true" level of mobility with respect to collective mobilization and individuals' assessment of risks and uncertainties.

In addition to reporting their self-assessed mobility, respondents were asked whether they had been unemployed in the last three months, in the last twelve months, or in the last five years. A score of 1 meant that the person had been unemployed or sought jobs during the specified period (i.e. three months, one year, or five years); if the respondent said they had not been unemployed for one of these durations, the variable was coded as 0. Furthermore, respondents were asked about the duration of the longest period of unemployment (in months) during the last three years.[13] Table 5 shows the results of an analysis that examines the association between self-perceived (im)mobility and the likelihood of being unemployed in a given period.

In the analysis, I also controlled for age in total years (older people may naturally be less mobile and in more secure jobs and hence less likely to be unemployed); gender (women along with younger people are arguably more

[13] The exact wording of the question was: "Thinking just of the last 3 years, what was the longest period in months, if any, that you were continuously unemployed and seeking work?"

Table 5 Immobility and spells of unemployment

Variables	Model 1 Variables Unemployment period (in total months)	Model 2 Been unemployed (last three months)	Model 3 Been unemployed (last twelve months)
Job mobility	-0.0807***	-0.0618***	-0.0633***
	(0.0152)	(0.00874)	(0.0112)
Gender	0.0132	0.00382	-0.307***
	(0.0703)	(0.0396)	(0.0517)
Age	-0.0294***	-0.0101***	0.0206***
	(0.00401)	(0.00231)	(0.00239)
Education	-0.0871***	-0.0437***	-0.0653***
	(0.0151)	(0.0117)	(0.0110)
Constant	3.781***	0.392	-0.290
	(0.360)	(0.242)	(0.241)
Observations	18,873	19,312	5,602
R-squared	0.016		

Notes: A regression analysis was performed for Model 1, with robust standard errors clustered across countries. A logistic regression was conducted for Models 2 and 3, with robust standard errors clustered across countries. Robust standard errors are shown in parentheses. ***$p < 0.01$, * $p < 0.05$, *$p < 0.1$.

prominently employed in temporary jobs and are therefore more vulnerable to unemployment); and total number of years of education (more educated people may be more skilled and less mobile but are also less likely to be unemployed). Gender was coded as 1 for male respondents and 0 for female respondents.

The results show that mobility – the ease of changing jobs and sectors – largely reduces the duration of unemployment. Individuals who assess themselves as being less mobile using the 10-point scale were also more likely to have endured longer periods of unemployment over the last three years compared to more mobile individuals (Model 1). A respondent who assessed their mobility with a score of 3 using the 10-point scale would have endured an unemployment period that was approximately two weeks longer compared with someone who assessed their mobility with a score of 8 using the same scale. Immobile individuals are also more likely to have been unemployed over the past three months (Model 2), over the past twelve months (Model 3), and over the past five years (not reported here because of space limitations). A 1-point decrease in the 10-point scale of self-assessed mobility increases the likelihood of unemployment by 6 percent. Thus, someone with a self-assessed mobility score of 3 was more than 30 percent more likely to have become unemployed in the past twelve months compared with someone with a self-assessed mobility score of 8. The impact of mobility on unemployment is also statistically highly significant. These results support the theory proposed in Section 3 that immobile individuals are much more vulnerable to potential unemployment. Once again, I do not interpret the control variables because of significant confounding issues related to control variables.

The theory proposed in this Element further stipulates that immobile individuals face greater economic hardship. The ESS respondents were asked whether they "had to manage on a lower household income in the last three years" and to rate the extent of their agreement with this statement using a 6-point scale, ranging from 0 (not at all) to 6 (a great deal). A second item was: "Which of the descriptions on this card comes closest to how you feel about your household's income nowadays?" Possible responses were: (1) "Living comfortably on present income," (2) "coping on present income," (3) "finding it difficult on present income," and (4) "finding it very difficult on present income." For both metrics, the variables were coded so that economic hardship increased with higher numbers on the scale. Using this survey data, I investigate whether economic hardship increases with job immobility, that is, whether individuals who reported being more immobile also reported going through more hardship during the Great Recession of 2010 in Europe. Table 6 shows the results of the analysis.

Controlling for education, gender, and age, immobile individuals reported undergoing greater economic hardship and income loss (managing on a lower income) than more mobile individuals. A 1-point decrease on the mobility scale increased the likelihood of hardship by 12 percent, with this impact also being statistically highly significant. The reason may be that immobile individuals stayed in their jobs even if their incomes were reduced because of the ongoing economic crisis. It would be difficult for them to find a job with similar benefits; hence they would be more likely to accept losses of income and rights. As the case studies in Section 5 reveal, many individuals switched to part-time contracts in Greece, while staying in their existing jobs with lower pay. Consequently, their economic hardship was compounded.

Lastly, I examine whether immobility affects the likelihood of individuals participating in lawful demonstrations. This analysis is once again based on data from the ESS survey, in which respondents were asked if they had "taken part in a lawful public demonstration" during the last twelve months. Affirmative responses were coded as 1 and negative responses as 0. The sample was restricted to countries that were under an IMF program

Table 6 (Im)mobility and household income during the economic crisis of 2010

Variables	Model 4 Perceived household income	Model 5 Managed on lower income
Job mobility	-0.113***	-0.0781***
	(0.0213)	(0.0141)
Sex	-0.284***	-0.295***
	(0.0471)	(0.0295)
Age	-0.0122***	-0.0148***
	(0.00362)	(0.00364)
Education	-0.117***	-0.0599***
	(0.0134)	(0.0118)
Observations	19,265	19,102

Notes: Ordered logistic regression with robust standard errors clustered across countries. Robust standard errors are shown in parentheses. ***$p < 0.01$, **$p < 0.05$, *$p < 0.1$.

when the survey was conducted, in line with the scope conditions of this study. Among the twenty-eight countries mentioned, those under an IMF program when the ESS was carried out were Greece, Hungary, Iceland, Ireland, Latvia, and Romania. Portugal concluded a program in the spring of 2011 after the survey was conducted in that country (between October 2010 and March 2011); therefore Portugal is not included in the sample. Regrettably, Iceland, Latvia, and Romania did not participate in the ESS Round 5. The final sample, therefore, includes Greece, Hungary, and Ireland. Table 7 depicts the results of the analysis on the likelihood of participation in a lawful demonstration during the past year dating back to the day of the interview and controlling for various demographic characteristics – trade union membership, and ideological self-placement on the left–right scale. The self-placement on the ideological scale was measured as 0 (far left) and 10 (far right).

The results show that mobility is negatively correlated with the likelihood of participation in demonstrations. Individuals who believe that it would be relatively easy to find a similar or better job if they lost their current job are less likely to participate in demonstrations. A 1-point increase in the 10-point mobility scale decreased the likelihood of participation in demonstrations by 2 percent. Hence, someone with a self-assessed score of 3 using this scale would be 10 percent more likely to participate in demonstrations than someone with a mobility score of 8 using the same scale. Furthermore, the impact is statistically very significant.

Table 7 (Im)mobility and participation in demonstrations

Variables	Model 6 Participation in a lawful demonstration
Job mobility	-0.0214***
	(0.00751)
Gender	0.373***
	(0.0705)
Age	0.0215*
	(0.0124)
Left–right scale	-0.286**
	(0.122)
Trade union member	1.124***
	(0.406)
Education	0.0896
	(0.0593)
Constant	-4.083**
	(1.738)
Observations	535

Notes: Logistic regression with robust standard errors clustered across countries in the sample. Robust standard errors are shown in parentheses. ***$p < 0.01$, **$p < 0.05$, *$p < 0.1$.

Regrettably, the survey did not include strike action, participation in industrial disputes, or other protest methods such as blocking roads, slowing down work, occupying buildings, sit-ins, and other forms of nonviolent or violent protest. Nevertheless, the analysis provides additional evidence that immobility could result in longer spells of unemployment, greater economic hardship, and an increased likelihood of participation in political protests. The case studies in the next section draw on interview data, selected leaders' speeches, and news reports on specific protests and strikes; they demonstrate the link between the shock of labor conditions in an immobile market and collective mobilization as a response. These case studies demonstrate how mobility functions as a tool of readjustment and a diffuser of social and labor market risks in some countries while preventing the rise of sudden outbursts of unrest.

5 European Borrowers of the Fund: Mobility, Conditionality, and Unrest

The economic recession in Europe in 2008 started with a spillover from the United States and later unfolded within the unique context of the European political economy. Macroeconomic imbalances between Northern European countries (lenders) and the peripheral countries of Europe (borrowers), in particular, were exposed at the start of the crisis. Northern European economies had been stagnant for a very long time and the returns to money there were low. Actors were incentivized to lend their money to peripheral countries (Copelovitch et al., 2016). This was made easier by the fact that they could do so free from exchange rate risks thanks to a single currency, the euro (Fuller and Jones, 2014). Inflation in the peripheral countries, on the other hand, was higher compared to the lending countries before the Great Recession and they were incentivized to borrow cheap credit at a favorable rate (Fuller and Jones, 2014). This system worked well for some time before the crisis until the liquidity was squeezed in the lenders' markets and the large budgetary deficits of peripheral countries were exposed and market confidence in them rapidly declined (Copelovitch et al., 2016). At the broadest level, these macroeconomic imbalances and the lending–borrowing dynamic caused the crisis in Europe. The crisis and the responses of labor markets and actors, however, were further shaped by national contexts, as will be discussed in this section.

At the height of the Great Recession in Europe, Greece borrowed from the IMF, the European Commission, and the European Central Bank (ECB) in May 2010. This was the second so-called Troika arrangement in the European Union following Latvia in 2008. After Greece, Ireland also concluded an agreement later in 2010, while Portugal joined the list in 2011.[14]

Comparison between the four European borrowers chosen is ideal for the purposes of this study; they demonstrate variability in terms of labor mobility and the expansiveness of the IMF's labor market reform conditions. Greece's labor market is profoundly immobile; Portugal's is moderately immobile; Ireland's labor market is moderately mobile; and Latvia is among the most mobile labor markets in the European sample. While Ireland and Portugal received relatively few (or no) labor market reform conditions, Greece and

[14] Note that the Troika arrangement is inconsequential for the purposes of this Element, since, as the previous section shows, a similar mechanism linking labor market reform conditions and immobility to labor unrest exists in a global selection of cases. Furthermore, as long as conditions are assigned, it is not of high importance whether they were primarily recommended by the Fund or the Commission (or Germany, for that matter). More than the conditions' source, their empirical and material impact on labor groups' existing and prospective income are consequential.

Table 8 Mobility and labor conditionality in Greece, Latvia, Ireland, and Portugal in the post-2008 crisis

		Labor market mobility	
		High	**Low**
IMF reform conditions	**Expansive**	Latvia, 2008	Greece, 2010
	Nonexpansive	Ireland, 2010	Portugal, 2011

Table 9 Collective bargaining coverage, unionization, and unemployment replacement ratio in Greece, Ireland, Latvia, and Portugal

Indicators/country	Greece	Ireland	Latvia	Portugal
Unionization rate	22.2%	31.6%	15.2%	18.6%
Collective bargaining coverage (% of workers)	100%	40.5%	34.2%	78.1%
Net replacement rate in unemployment	41%	62%	80%	75%

Source: OECD data on trade unionization, collective bargaining coverage, and net replacement rate datasets. https://stats.oecd.org/.

Notes: Data refer to the first year of the respective structural adjustment program, hence 2010 for Greece and Ireland; 2011 for Portugal; and 2008 for Latvia. Collective bargaining coverage data for Ireland is from 2009 and for Latvia from 2006 due to data unavailability.

Latvia received very high numbers of reform conditions. The four European borrowers can be depicted in a two-by-two matrix of conditionality and mobility as in Table 8.

Furthermore, these four countries demonstrate significant variance in terms of their institutional settings and how their labor markets are organized, (dis) empowering different actors in the rise of contentious action. In particular, Ireland and Latvia have a more liberal orientation, relegating most wage-setting and employment relations to the market (Ó Riain, 2014), whereas Greece and Portugal have a tendency toward more dualized labor markets with several very well-protected sectors such as the public sector and those where there is minimal to no regulation (e.g., the construction sector) (Papapetrou, 2006; Magone, 2014). Table 9 summarizes some aspects of wage coordination, unemployment benefits, and trade unionization in the four cases.

Table 9 shows that all four countries had low unionization rates at the start of their programs. Surprisingly, Ireland had the highest trade union density, that is, the percentage of eligible salaried workers who are union members. The four countries demonstrate significant variation in terms of collective bargaining coverage. Two Southern European states, Greece and Portugal, have very high coverage, that is a very high percentage of workers benefiting from collective wage bargaining. Comparatively, Ireland and Latvia have lower rates. In Latvia and Portugal, workers had a greater fallback option with high rates of unemployment benefit – 80 percent and 75 percent of their last salaries respectively – whereas Greek workers had the lowest replacement rate at 41 percent. We can argue that workers in Portugal and Greece, especially the latter, would have been very sensitive to labor market flexibilization measures and the dismantling of collective wage institutions.

In addition to demonstrating variance across independent variables, the study of these four countries significantly contributes to our knowledge of IMF programs. The European borrowers are among the richest democracies in the world and show significant similarities in terms of their development levels controlling for unobserved confounding variables. More importantly, until now, scholars have studied unrest and violent repression under IMF programs only in developing countries. The study of labor unrest in relatively more developed cases provides great analytical leverage into the causal mechanism; the institutional, political, and economic weaknesses that plague developing countries would not be observable to a similar extent in richer, democratic countries. Therefore, these cases demonstrate the adjustment mechanisms that mobility provides and the strong reactions that arise when labor mobility is low and adjustment opportunities are either minimal or nonexistent. Greece, in 2010, in particular, shows the labor grievances that can be caused by labor conditions in a largely immobile labor market.

5.1 Greece in 2010: Immobility and Labor Unrest

The economic crisis in Greece started with the revelation of large public debt following the September 2009 elections. Once Greece's true budget deficit was exposed, which was three times higher than the eurozone criteria, market confidence rapidly deteriorated. Panic that Greece would not be able to repay its debt to its creditors ensued. Government bond spreads rapidly increased in the last quarter of 2009 and the beginning of 2010, and the government became effectively unable to borrow from the private markets. Greece's crisis was essentially a sovereign debt crisis created by years of depending on cheap credit from Northern European countries to Greece for higher returns. It was, however, made even more painful due to the revelation that earlier government statistics were distorted and not accurate (Fuller and Jones, 2014). This harmed market confidence even further, unlike the other three cases discussed here. Under these conditions, Greece signed the first bailout package on May 5, 2010, agreeing to borrow 110 billion euros (80 billion from the ECB and the European Commission as well as a bilateral agreement with EU countries, and 30 billion euros from the IMF) over three years (European Commission Directorate-General for Economic and Financial Affairs, 2010). Immediately after signing the agreement, Greece experienced a sudden and dramatic rise in contentious action.

The phrase "The cradle of democracy rocking the world" was used by historian Mark Mazower to describe the aftermath of Greece's signing of the IMF agreement (Mazower, 2011). Forty-four strikes, twelve of which were general strikes, and numerous labor protests took place between 2010 and 2013, following the signing of the agreement.[15] The protests were often synchronized with negotiations with the IMF and European institutions, and with votes on bills (specified in the program) in parliament. One of the biggest demonstrations over the three years was organized before votes were held on the labor conditionality bills (promising wage cuts, changes to pension rights, and layoffs of civil servants) in the Greek parliament on October 19, 2011, when more than 80,000 people gathered in Syntagma Square in Athens (Donadio and Kitsantonis, 2011). Several months earlier, on May 11, 2011, a similarly large demonstration (with 20,000 people participating) had been organized by the public sector union ADEDY[16] and the private sector union GSEE[17] during negotiations between the Greek government and the Troika institutions (Maltezou and Melander, 2011). On other occasions, thousands gathered in Athens and in smaller cities such as Thessaloniki to protest the agreement and the measures included in the programs. Strikes almost froze life in Greece during that period. Compared to Ireland, Latvia, and Portugal, Greece also had by far the greatest number of workdays lost because of industrial disputes. Figure 6 shows the number of days lost due to strike activity in the four countries.

Figure 6 shows that strikes in Greece were more intensive than in the other three countries and also had a greater impact on the economy and labor relations. This was not, however, because of a few, long-lasting strikes but because of a very large number of short strikes. The majority of strikes lasted between two hours and two days. The most common were twenty-four-hour strikes. Almost all sectors of the labor market ranging from prison workers to doctors,

[15] Nexis database, various years. https://LexisNexis.com/NexisUni.

[16] Ανωτατη Διοίκηση Ενώσεων Δημοσίων Υπαλλήλων (Congress of Public Administration Employees).

[17] Γενική Συνομοσπονδία Εργατών Ελλάδος (General Confederation of Greek Workers).

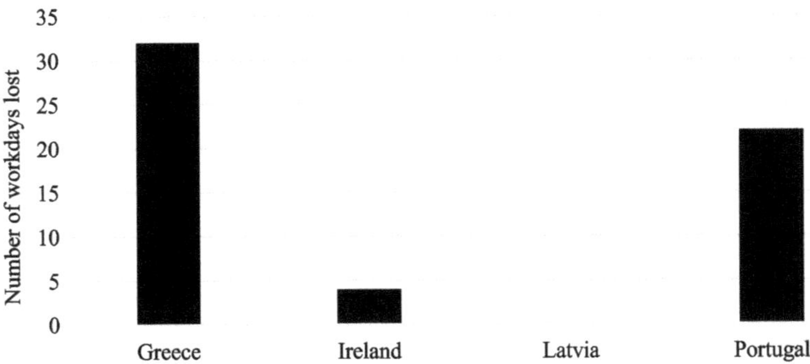

Figure 6 Number of workdays lost due to industrial disputes per 1,000 salaried workers

Sources: For Ireland (2012), Latvia (2011), and Portugal (2013): OECD industrial disputes data (www.oecd.org/els/emp/Industrial-disputes.pdf). For Greece (2012): author's calculation based on a strike activity report published in 2013 by the GSEE's (private sector umbrella union) Labor Institute (Katsoridas and Lambousaki, 2013). The report documents strike activity and the number of hours that work stoppages lasted. Data for the duration of some strike activity (approximately 20 percent) are not available. Therefore, the numbers should be taken as an approximation and not the precise number of workdays lost. Greek authorities have not reported official industrial dispute data since 1999.

engineers to journalists, social workers, archaeologists, educators, radio technicians, hotel workers, Coca-Cola workers, and workers at PASOK's headquarters – the party in government – participated in the strike action (Katsoridas and Lambousaki, 2013). Journalists, radio station employees, metal manufacturing workers, station guards, restaurant workers, and a multitude of private sector workers struck against dismissals and wage reductions, demanding collective wage bargaining (Katsoridas and Lambousaki, 2013). There were a few exceptions to these short strikes, however. In 2012, 18 out of 439 strikes recorded by GSEE lasted more than forty-eight hours. In one of them, tourist bus drivers struck for four days in June 2012, requesting the signing of a sectoral collective labor agreement. In another strike, in September 2012, sewage workers struck for seven days with repeated three-hour work stoppages against wage cuts (Katsoridas and Lambousaki, 2013).

A novel element that can be noted in the protests between 2010 and 2012 is the political, social, and ideological heterogeneity of the protestor groups, and the secondary roles played by more frequent protestors (such as leftist organizations and anarchist groups) (Karyotis and Rüdig, 2018). The protestors came from diverse socioeconomic backgrounds and income groups within Greek society (Psimitis, 2011). Additionally, leftist organizations and anarchist groups, which historically had led the protest movement in Greece

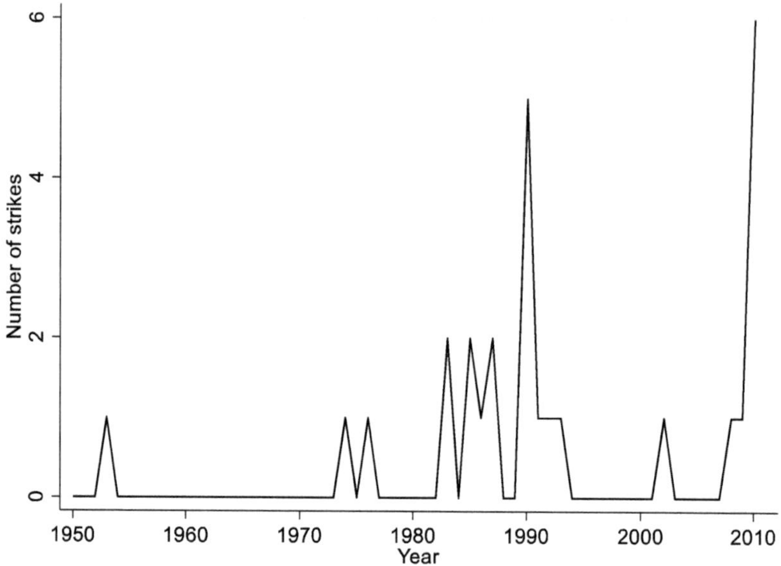

Figure 7 Frequency of strikes in Greece between 1950 and 2010
Source: CNTS dataset (Banks, 2008).

(Andronikidou and Kovras, 2012), seemed to assume secondary roles during the 2010–12 protests (Psimitis, 2011; Aslanidis, 2016; Karyotis and Rüdig, 2018).[18] Aslanidis (2016) attributes the heterogeneity of the protestors, new groups joining in, and subdued roles for leftist organizations in 2010 to the goal of deliberate populist mobilization by organizers of the protests. Psimitis (2011), on the other hand, suggests that the political unrest in Greece can be analyzed through the lenses of a "new protest cycle" in which nontraditional protestor groups were activated. Although both authors offer plausible explanations for the heterogeneity of the groups, a closer investigation reveals that 2010 was not a first; there was similar sudden surge in strike frequency in 1990. Figure 7 depicts the historical trend in strike frequency in Greece between 1990 and 2010.

Figure 7 shows that after a period of less frequent strikes in the 2000s, there was a sudden surge in industrial action in 2010. A similar spike is observable in 1990. Both the years 1990 and 2010 were periods of extensive structural reform in Greece. The 1990 reforms were also initiated under an emergency loan from the European Community to meet the urgent financing needs of the government and to conduct fiscal consolidation and labor market structural reforms,

[18] For a very concise and insightful discussion on the role of mass protests and the culture of protest in Greece, see Andronikidou and Kovras (2012). For a more detailed discussion of the Greek left, specifically communism, see Kalyvas and Marantzidis (2002).

particularly under the Mitsotakis government (Trantidis, 2014). The summer of 1990 was also a period of labor unrest in Greece. What seems common to both periods is reform under external influence in a largely immobile market. When wage cuts, dismissals, and benefit cuts affect almost all sectors, the "fire" spreads everywhere.

When extensive labor conditions suddenly and sharply opened a largely immobile labor market this created large-scale grievances for diverse groups and triggered substantial labor unrest in Greece, activating new groups in 2010. The IMF labor conditions in the Greek program were aimed at bringing greater flexibility into the labor market. They were targeted toward "micro flexibility, namely the ability of the economy to allow for the reallocation of workers to jobs needed to sustain growth; and macro flexibility, namely the ability of the economy to adjust to macroeconomic shocks" (Blanchard et al., 2014, p. 4). This translates into employing workers where they can be most productive and enhancing the ability of market forces to determine wage levels. Collective agreements and a high minimum wage are believed to distort market conditions and set wages above the optimum level. Moreover, employment protections such as making firing and hiring difficult, discouraging part-time work, and high overtime payments were argued to make the labor market rigid for new entrants and to hamper growth.[19]

Labor is profoundly immobile in Greece. Indeed, formal job tenure is the highest among twenty OECD countries.[20] Similarly, labor mobility levels – the number of worker changes between sectors – are half of the OECD average (in 2009, only 0.2 percent moved across sectors in Greece compared to 5 percent in Latvia). At the macro-level, the IMF argued that such rigidities reduced the competitiveness of the Greek economy, discouraged exports due to high labor costs, and deterred investment (again, due to high labor costs associated with production) (IMF News, 2011).

In the case of Greece, we can explain labor immobility by well-developed job and wage protection institutions, as well as uneven and unequal social protection between the public, private, and informal sectors, that is, labor market segmentation. Before the changes under the Troika program, Greece had three layers of collective bargaining institutions: the national level between the umbrella trade union and the employers' associations, in addition to sectoral and firm-level bargaining. Based on the *principe de faveur,* the most favorable level applied to individual cases (Koukiadaki and Kretsos, 2012; Patra, 2012).

[19] IMF Request for Stand-By Arrangement, 2010. https://doi.org/10.5089/9781455206902.002.

[20] Whereas 30.9 percent of Greeks reported being in their current job for fewer than six months in 2007, before the financial crisis, the percentage was considerably higher in Ireland in the same year (43.5 percent). OECD, various years. https://stats.oecd.org/Index.aspx?DataSetCode=TENURE_AVE.

In addition, labor institutions were strong, controlling almost every aspect of a member's working life. Collective agreements, established with Law 1876/1990, regulated working conditions including working hours; time limitations; type of contracts (e.g., part-time, fixed-term, and short-term contracts) and their duration and conditions; minimum wage; and overtime payments (Patra, 2012). In the case of a dispute, workers could unilaterally apply to the arbitration authority, the Greek Mediation and Arbitration Service (OMED), and challenge set wage levels, whereas employer associations did not have the same right. In other words, labor institutions in Greece gave social partners a strong role outside the legislative process and provided strict employment and wage protection. However, such protection did not extend to all sectors.

The second reason for labor immobility in the Greek labor market is significant wage differentials and differences in employment protection between the public, private, and informal sectors as well as between part-time and full-time work. In fact, there seem to be three different labor markets operating side by side in the country. The first distinction is between public and private sector jobs, where there are significant wage differentials, in favor of public sector jobs (Papapetrou, 2006; Christopoulou and Monastiriotis, 2016). Second, part-time work is considerably disadvantaged compared to full-time jobs. Finally, there is a considerable unregulated and unregistered shadow market in Greece, where social protection is absent (Prosser, 2016). These significant differences in wages and protections make the labor market less mobile; mobility increases the risk of falling into the "less privileged" sector. More than that, it compounds risks in the case of flexibilization measures.

Labor conditionality imposed by the IMF was an exogenous shock to the immobile Greek labor market. First, labor conditionality reduced existing employment protection measures, and diminished the security that insider labor enjoyed. For instance, the notice period for laying off workers was reduced by half (Koukiadaki and Kretsos, 2012). The maximum duration for fixed-term contracts was extended from twelve to thirty-six months. The minimum wage for young people (under twenty years of age) was set at 80 percent of the national minimum wage, and for new entrants above twenty-five years of age at 84 percent (Koukiadaki and Kretsos, 2012). Moreover, the collective bargaining process has been decentralized. In addition to the three-layered bargaining process, which had been sidelined by legislative acts, "associations of persons" (as opposed to unions) were given the right to negotiate wage and employment conditions with employers. The duration of part-time and short-term work contracts and their maximum number of renewals have been extended. The definition of part-time work has been increased to forty hours per week, and overtime payments has been changed into hourly rates in the contract, abolishing the previously defined "ten percent extra" rule for overtime work (Patra, 2012, p. 16). These measures not only reduced the incomes of insider workers, but also increased their risks (for a full list of labor conditions in Greece, see Appendix II).

The IMF's labor market conditions led to three types of risk for immobile workers in Greece. First, employment protection declined. Existing jobs have become less secure since hiring and firing became easier. This also led to a rapid decline in employment across all sectors (see Table 10). In immobile markets such as Greece, the reallocation process is slow, and flexibility measures result in a decline in employment levels in the short term. Conversely, in mobile labor markets, we either observe movement toward growing sectors, despite the crisis, or different sectors peaking at different points during the crisis and absorbing redundant workers, thus preventing a drastic decline in employment in the short term. Table 10 depicts the number of employees across eight sectors in the Greek economy between 2009 and 2012.

Table 10 shows a decline in employment across all sectors between 2010 and 2012. This is not necessarily the result of the economic crisis, however. As will be illustrated by the Irish and the Latvian cases, and to a certain extent in Portugal, employment does not collapse in more mobile labor markets. It continues to grow in sectors that are expanding, despite the crisis, while shrinking in others. The adjustment process is also much quicker in mobile labor markets, preventing a steady decline in employment. Both the collapse of employment and the rise in unemployment were even more painful in Greece compared to the other three cases, because Greece had the lowest net replacement ratio in 2010 – 41 percent.[21]

Second, as a result of the Troika program, wage protections were reduced by promoting individual contracts as opposed to collective ones. This change led to an immediate decline in nominal wages for those who were still in work. In particular, the dismantling of collective bargaining institutions and cancellation of the automatic extension of sectoral agreements for those not represented in negotiations hurt almost all groups in the labor market. In Greece, collective agreement coverage declined from 100 percent in 2010, when the Troika agreement was signed, to 51.5 percent in 2012 and further to 37.3 percent in 2013 after several changes to labor law.[22]

With the labor law changes under the Troika program, involuntary part-time work, a common indicator of precarity in the labor market

[21] OECD Net Replacement Rate in Unemployment dataset. https://stats.oecd.org/Index.aspx?DataSetCode=NRR.

[22] OECD Collective Bargaining Coverage dataset. https://stats.oecd.org/index.aspx?DataSetCode=CBC.

Table 10 Number of employees across sectors in Greece, 2009–2012

Sector/year	2010	2011	2012
Agriculture; forestry and fishing	535,408	491,391	471,424
Mining and quarrying	13,060	10,987	10,871
Manufacturing	460,714	402,098	344,805
Utilities	57,716	49,540	46,946
Construction	314,476	241,245	197,104
Wholesale and retail trade; repair of motor vehicles and motorcycles	786,441	738,299	651,166
Transport; storage and communication	290,601	266,805	245,292
Accommodation and food service activities	303,486	290,194	266,998
Financial and insurance activities	113,886	111,635	109,006
Real estate; business and administrative activities	294,300	291,425	285,611
Public administration and defence; compulsory social security	363,959	348,290	320,523
Education	316,561	298,723	284,814
Human health and social work activities	241,938	233,778	219,309
Other services	226,523	204,734	171,323

Source: ILO Employment Statistics. https://ilostat.ilo.org/data/.

Note: Employee numbers in thousands.

(Rueda, 2012, 2014; Prosser, 2016), increased. According to OECD data, the share of involuntary part-time workers as a percentage of the total labor force increased from 2.2 percent in 2009 to 4 percent in 2013. In 2013, 61.3 percent of all part-time workers said that they were involuntarily in part-time work.[23] In Latvia, for instance, in the same year, the comparable statistic was 37.9 percent. Moreover, there was a considerable increase in overtime work (especially for part-time workers), and a visible shift from full-time to part-time work for existing workers, with reduced wages and lower levels of overtime payments.[24] With lower levels of protection and without the prospect of a job with similar benefits, Greek workers stayed in their jobs despite the reduced benefits.

Figure 8 shows the quarterly data for the total number of workers in part-time and full-time work. It shows that during the period, while full-time work declined, part-time contracts increased, despite a collapse in employment. This suggests that most workers stayed in their jobs and switched to part-time

[23] OECD Incidence of Involuntary Part Time Workers. https://stats.oecd.org/Index.aspx?DataSetCode=INVPT_I.

[24] ELSTAT, various years. www.statistics.gr/en/home/.

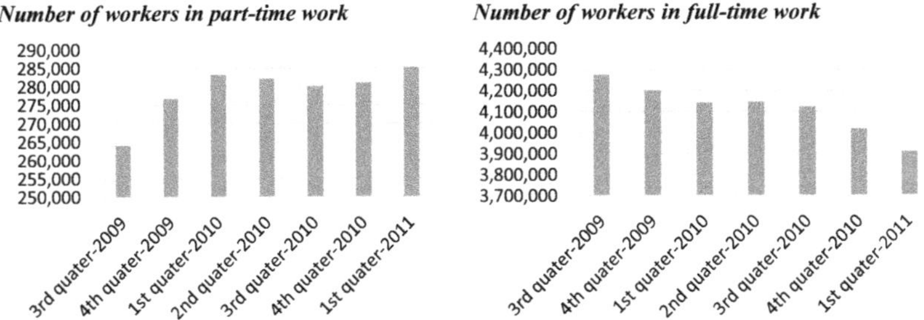

Figure 8 Number of employees in part-time and full-time work in Greece, 2009–2011

Source: Hellenic Statistical Authority (various years).

contracts. Indeed, union representatives of the GSEE confirmed that when firing became easier, many workers were fired and later reemployed in the same job on a part-time contract (Appendix III, Interview No. 1). In other words, many workers did not move to jobs where they would be more efficient as envisaged by the flexibilization measures. Instead, they stayed in their jobs with reduced benefits.

Third, there is evidence that labor market reform conditions paved the way for expansion of an already strong informal market, under the threat of dismissals and individual contracts in Greece. Informal employment agreements and individual-level agreements (instead of collective ones) increased (Patra, 2012, p. 23; Dedoussopoulos et al., 2013, p. 44). In other words, the labor market did not respond to the changes by shifting and reallocating workers to where they would be the most productive. Instead, there was a loss of rights and income for groups of workers, who were "stuck" in their existing jobs, and an overall decline in employment in the short term.

Prosser (2016, p. 962) explains that the decades-long dualization trend was turned into a liberalization trend in Greece under forceful external pressure for reform and paved the way for increased precarity in the labor market. In other words, historical institutional reform trends changed track under the Troika reforms. This, of course, did not happen without labor resistance.

The trade unions took a leadership role in organizing protests and strikes in Greece. At times, they organized joint strikes. Following meetings with the IMF, EC, ECB officials and the prime minister on April 27, 2010, GSEE President Giannis Panagopoulos stated that his members would resist the labor measures through strong action, not excluding strikes, thus "sending a strong message of protest to both the government and the IMF, the European Central Bank, and the European Commission" (GSEE, 2010).

One question is: Why were they so successful in mobilizing such large-scale groups? When interpreted in the context of the extensiveness of labor market reforms and the economic hardship and grievances they caused in the labor market, and the activation of new groups in the protests and strikes, we can argue that the sudden rise of hardship due to large-scale immobility provided the basis on which the trade unions could rally members and nonmembers alike.

Another remaining question is: What did political authority do when there was such a rise in contentious action and demands placed on them? Former Minister of Labor Louka Katseli and former Finance Minister George Papaconstantinou, who also negotiated the first program, argued that they knew the labor conditions would lead to a collapse of employment without bringing added flexibility (Appendix III, Interviews No. 2 and No. 3). However, they also argued that the Troika partners did not listen to them. The scientific director of GSEE, George Argeitis, explained that the trade union specifically proposed increased public works as a reintegration strategy for redundant workers, but received a negative response (Appendix III, Interview No. 1). Then Minister of Finance Papaconstantinou, on the other hand, admitted that the government was aware of the possibility of a rapid decline in wages, due to relaxation of the wage-bargaining institutions, and rising unemployment; however, it was not able to react due to the tight budgetary cuts in public spending (Appendix III, Interview No. 3).

The issue at the core of the lending, the government's urgent need for external finance, skewed the relationship between the Troika and the Greek government toward the former. The government was under a pressing need for liquidity, which enhanced IMF conditionality and its impact on policy-making. As a result, the PASOK government – a center-left, social-democratic party in power – experienced a rift between the dual roles of governing party (as the executive) and a political party representing its constituency. Ministers stated that they met with party cadres several times to explain the program (Appendix III, Interview No. 2 and No. 3). Then Minister of Finance Papaconstantinou explained that there was a large group of PASOK MPs who were against the program. He justified the Party's choice in implementing the program, however, believing it was necessary and part of the responsibility of government. Later, PASOK paid the price by losing much of its voter base in the first elections following the agreement. The party received around 13 percent of the vote in two elections in 2012 (in May and in June) and lost 199 seats in the parliament compared to the 2009 elections that brought it to power.

Greece is sometimes considered a recalcitrant case, where implementation of the IMF program was slow and often incomplete, especially compared to Ireland during the same period. Niamh Hardiman and colleagues (2019) explains this as lack of "country ownership" in Greece compared to high ownership in Ireland and a modest level of country ownership in Portugal. However, this can also be interpreted once again in terms of the clash between the existing institutional setup in Greece and the IMF's "template." As will be discussed in Sections 5.2 and 5.3, the liberal political economies, Latvia and Ireland, had less of a clash with the market-based policy prescriptions of the IMF. Portugal had a lower reaction to the IMF because the program there was more slowly paced and less front-loaded, partly because of the lessons learned in Greece. In Greece, the combination – sudden and forceful deregulation and a largely immobile, segmented labor market – was explosive.

With democratic channels blocked, except for elections, labor groups in Greece organized to block the implementation of the program. Confirming this point, contentious action significantly declined in Greece after the 2012 elections and again further after the 2015 elections. The scientific director of GSEE, George Argeitis, puts it succinctly: "Labor flexibility is catastrophic for labor, for our institutions, for our society, and so we [GSEE] reacted and tried to block its implementation" (Appendix III, Interview No. 1). Ireland, on the other hand, tells a different story.

5.2 Ireland in 2010: Mobility and Adjustment

Ireland realigned its economy toward exports, free trade, and attracting foreign investment during its "Celtic Tiger" years in the 1990s and early 2000s (Ó Riain, 2014; Cannon and Murphy, 2015). The strategy "worked" and, during this period, Ireland's economy grew exponentially. This "good fortune," however, came to an end in 2008. The sudden decline in Ireland's exports, the drying up of foreign investment, and the exposure of Irish banks to international assets led to a crisis at home in Ireland's small and open economy.[25] In parallel with international markets, the housing bubble was exposed leading to a considerable deceleration in house prices and the contraction of the construction sector.[26] Bank recapitalizations, nationalizations, and bank restructuring placed a considerable burden on the government budget. The current account balance of the government rapidly deteriorated. Between 2008 and 2010 GDP per capita income declined by 20 percent.[27] In December 2010, the Irish government concluded an agreement with the European Commission and the ECB amounting to 45 billion euro, and an Extended Fund Facility (EFF) agreement with the IMF amounting to 22.5 billion euro over three years (IMF Press Release, 2010).

[25] IMF Article IV Consultation Report, 2012. www.imf.org/external/pubs/ft/scr/2012/cr12264.pdf.

[26] IMF Article IV Consultation Report, 2009. https://bit.ly/3GHFuiz.

[27] World Bank (various years). https://data.worldbank.org/indicator/NY.GDP.PCAP.CD?end=2012&locations=IE&start=2008.

The loan conditions set in the agreement with the Troika institutions focused on the financial sector and bank recapitalizations and fiscal consolidation in Ireland. The government established the National Assets Management Agency (NAMA) and used the personal pension fund (founded as a safety net for the aging population of Ireland) for crisis adjustment and to balance the government budget.[28] The loan program set government expenditure ceilings and limited external borrowing.[29]

There were no formal labor market conditions in the program, unlike in Greece. However, before the program was signed, the minimum wage had already been cut; the government reduced social welfare benefits; government pensions for new entrants to the labor market were decreased; and income tax was increased.[30] Approximately 25,000 public sector jobs were cut (Burns, 2010). In other words, a considerable economic burden was placed on the population.

However, there were not many sustained protests or strikes in Ireland (Cannon and Murphy, 2015). For the program duration (2010–13), there were three major protests held in Dublin and other big cities on November 27, 2010 (Burns, 2010), December 5, 2010 (Reuters, 2009), and February 9, 2013 (ICTU, 2013). The November protest focused on the government budgetary cuts. The Irish Congress of Trade Unions (ICTU) called for an end to budget cuts and defended proemployment policies (ICTU, 2011). In the second one, protestors demanded a more gradual budgetary adjustment and to bring the deficit in line with EU rules by 2017 instead of the earlier date of 2013 (Reuters, 2009). In the third protest, the ICTU called for restructuring of the government's debt. The Congress argued that the debt burden, mostly due to bank restructuring and recapitalizations, put an uneven burden on Irish taxpayers and called for a reduction in the debt to European institutions. There was a national public sector service strike on November 24, 2010, with the participation of approximately 25,000 public sector workers, against public sector pay and pension cuts (Irish Times, 2009).

Observers sometimes view Ireland as an anomaly in terms of broad acquiescence and lack of protest under its Troika program (Pappas and O'Malley, 2014; Cannon and Murphy, 2015). Indeed, Nobel-winning economist Joseph Stiglitz reportedly stated that he was "astonished at [the] Irish ability to suck up austerity pain" (O'Hora, 2013). When comparing the differing reactions of labor groups in Greece and Ireland, scholars argue that there is a prevalent protest culture in Greece (Lee, 2021) whereas Ireland does not have one. This,

[28] IMF Article IV Consultation Report, 2009. https://bit.ly/3GHFuiz.

[29] IMF Letter of Intent, 2010. www.imf.org/external/np/loi/2010/irl/120310.pdf.

[30] Ibid.

Table 11 Number of employees across sectors in Ireland, 2010–2012

Sector/year	**2010**	**2011**	**2012**
Agriculture; forestry and fishing	111,058	108,842	109,327
Mining and quarrying	7,129	5,739	6,381
Manufacturing	217,696	215,085	211,943
Utilities	23,855	21,879	18,620
Construction	100,439	88,979	83,926
Wholesale and retail trade; repair of motor vehicles and motorcycles	282,811	278,663	276,758
Transport; storage and communication	176,217	178,674	178,332
Accommodation and food service activities	130,849	120,638	124,522
Financial and insurance activities	95,018	94,525	92,888
Real estate; business and administrative activities	192,616	198,084	195,200
Public administration and defence; compulsory social security	94,962	91,685	88,806
Education	144,140	138,631	138,780
Human health and social work activities	253,470	257,125	258,071
Other services	99,998	102,140	105,932

Source: ILO Employment Statistics. https://bit.ly/41HzOhW.

Note: Number of employees in thousands.

however, is not true. Ireland had a very strong labor movement and wage militancy until the start of the "Celtic Tiger" years (Hardiman, 1988; Culpepper and Regan, 2014). With a fundamental shift to export orientation and a "flexible developmental state," the economy was restructured during those years (Ó Riain, 2014) contributing to increased labor mobility.

In Ireland, employment or wages did not collapse to a similar degree as they did in Greece during the structural adjustment program. Mobile labor groups adjusted to the crisis by switching jobs and sectors.[31] In the Irish job market, we see an increase in the number of workers across different sectors between 2010 and 2012, indicating that workers were switching jobs and sectors (see Table 11).

For instance, employment in wholesale and retail trade; education; and accommodation and food service activities significantly declined in 2011 compared to 2010. In 2011, employment in real estate, business and administrative activities and human health and social work activities, on the other hand, increased despite the crisis. Yet, in 2012 human health and social work activities

[31] Ireland had an average mobility score of 0.019 between the years 1984 and 2007.

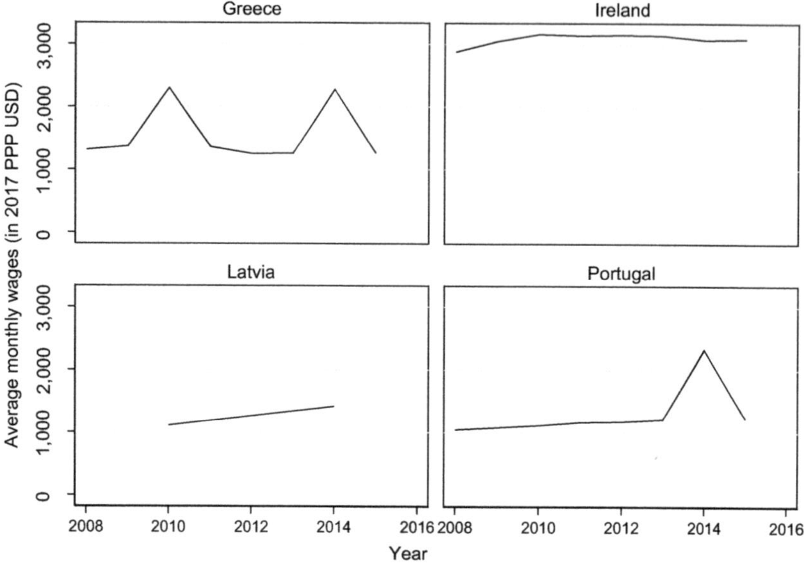

Figure 9 Aggregate monthly wages between 2008 and 2015 in Greece, Ireland, Latvia, and Portugal

Source: ILO Statistics on wages. https://bit.ly/41HzOhW.

continued to expand, in addition to employment in accommodation and food service activities and the broad category of "other services."[32]

Ireland demonstrates a very interesting pattern of mobility: different sectors peak in terms of employment, absorbing redundant workers and preventing a sharp decline in employment at different points during the crisis, unlike Greece in 2010. In this way, mobility also prevents substantial declines in wages and benefits for workers.[33] Table 11 depicts a fluctuation in the number of workers across different sectors. Unlike Greece, where we observed a secular decline in employment in the first two years of the crisis, in Ireland we see that some sectors peak in one year, and the next year employment declines in that sector while picking up again in another one. In mobile markets, workers have the possibility of moving across sectors and jobs if job opportunities decline in their sector.

Similarly, wages did not collapse in Ireland despite the public sector and minimum wage cuts. Figure 9 shows that average aggregate monthly wages in Ireland remained stable between 2008 and 2015, hovering around 3,000 US dollars (in purchasing power parity [PPP] in 2017 US dollars), whereas Greece

[32] ILO Employment statistics. https://bit.ly/41HzOhW.

[33] Data from the Irish Central Statistics Office (CSO). www.cso.ie/en/databases/.

experienced a dramatic decline in wages in 2011 after the structural adjustment program was signed in May 2010. Wages later zigzagged significantly in Greece between 2010 and 2014. In Latvia – another highly mobile labor market – there was a modest increase in wages between 2010 and 2014. In Portugal, wages suddenly increased in 2014 with a sharp decrease in 2015 (a return to the same level as in 2013) with the introduction of labor market changes under its structural adjustment program (the response of another highly immobile labor market to labor market reforms under a structural adjustment program). This was, in part, because wages in dualized labor markets are very responsive to changes in labor law. In addition, mobility and viable employment options with similar or better income and benefits outside their existing jobs provide some negotiating power to workers vis-à-vis employers.

High levels of mobility in the Irish economy can be explained by three factors: a highly skilled labor force, integration into the world economy, and reorganization of the economy around services during the Celtic Tiger years. Ireland has a highly educated workforce. In 2011, 47.53 percent of the Irish population between the ages of twenty-five and thirty-four were university graduates. This is the highest level among EU countries and especially high when compared to the percentage of university graduates within the population in Greece and Portugal in the same age group – 29.60 and 23.34 percent, respectively.[34] It can be argued that having a well-educated population has shifted the Irish economy toward the services sector and the production of high-end technological products, creating opportunities to change sectors and jobs within these broad categories (Yusuf and Nabeshima, 2012). While employment in manufacturing and construction consistently declined between 2010 and 2012, there were fluctuations in the broad services categories, especially in administrative, business, and communications-based jobs. High job specialization at the high end of skilled production can be seen as enforcing mobility.

A second factor that explains the absence of large-scale protests and strikes in Ireland is the broad overlap between the liberal orientation of the political economy in the country and the Troika policies. Market-based ideas enjoy broad legitimacy in Ireland (Ó Riain, 2014; Cannon and Murphy, 2015; Hardiman and Metinsoy, 2019). Unlike Greece, there was no clash between the broad institutional setup in the country and the policy prescriptions of the Troika.

Given this background, trade unions in Ireland found it harder to mobilize support for strikes and collective action, unlike in Greece. For example, the

[34] OECD Population with Tertiary Education database, 2023. http://data.oecd.org/eduatt/population-with-tertiary-education.htm#indicator-chart.

education sector took a serious hit during the crisis. Around 1,000 teachers lost their jobs (Irish Times, 2009). However, 84 percent of members of the Teachers' Union of Ireland (TUI) voted against striking in a ballot (Irish Examiner, 2010).

To be sure, Ireland also witnessed a party system collapse similar to that in Greece in the first post-program elections in 2011. The long-standing dominance of Fianna Fáil in the Irish political system (Murphy and Farrell, 2002) came to an end in the February 2011 elections. The party experienced a substantial decline in the share of votes and lost its parliamentary majority (Culpepper and Regan, 2014). However, the country did not go through a political implosion as Greece did under its Troika program. Even though groups such as public sector workers expressed their grievances in strike action and three large demonstrations, protests did not spread, thus activating large groups. Instead, workers relied on mobility to maintain employment and wages. Latvia further demonstrates the responsiveness of a mobile labor market to expansive labor market reforms, complementing the discussion on Ireland.

5.3 Latvia in 2008: Labor Conditions in a Mobile Market

The macroeconomic crisis started in Latvia in 2008 with the onset of the global financial crisis in the United States. At the time, Latvia had a currency peg and the Latvian Lat was fixed to the euro due to anticipated membership of the eurozone in 2014.[35] With the start of the crisis in global markets, the inflow of capital to Latvia stopped while, at the same time, a substantial amount of Latvian Lat was converted to euros at the given (favorable) exchange rate. A continuous injection of foreign currency into banks by the government became unsustainable over a long period. The Latvian government borrowed an exceptional amount – 1.7 billion euros (1,200 times its quota in the Fund) – from the IMF on December 23, 2008.[36] The Standby Agreement was cofinanced by the European Commission and the ECB.

The crisis in Latvia, similar to that in Ireland, started in the financial sector and later spilled over to the real economy (unlike in Greece and Portugal where the crises were primarily due to large budget deficits). Furthermore, both Latvia and Ireland are small and open economies with a primary export orientation (Regan, 2012; Mabbett and Schelkle, 2015). Finally, like Ireland, Latvia has a market-oriented political economy (Prosser, 2016). The country very rapidly became one of the most liberal economies in the world after independence following the collapse of the Soviet Union in 1991 (Feldmann, 2000). Bērziņš (2014, p. 89) suggests that policy-makers in Latvia perhaps distorted the idea of

[35] IMF Article IV Consultation, 2010. www.imf.org/external/pubs/ft/scr/2010/cr10356.pdf.

[36] Ibid.

liberalism to the point of "market anarchy," where all social problems are expected to be solved by the market.

Despite its highly liberal labor market, Latvia, as an anomaly, faced painful and highly intrusive labor market conditions after borrowing from the Fund in 2008. Minimum wage cuts, pension cuts, and public sector wage reductions and layoffs (Andritzky et al., 2021, p. 22) disproportionately affected labor groups. This is because the Latvian authorities wanted to keep the currency peg and the Troika program substituted external currency devaluation with internal labor market measures. Labor market reform conditions attached to the structural adjustment program were aimed at reducing unit labor costs, boosting competitiveness, and increasing exports to ensure recovery.[37] A "Committee to Promote Wage Restraint" was established for this purpose as part of the structural adjustment program.[38] This anomaly helps us in studying how a largely mobile labor market reacted to strict and extensive IMF-sponsored labor market reforms.

The crisis and labor market changes at first created an external shock for the Latvian job market. Similar to Greece, the unemployment rate increased. In particular, construction workers were disproportionately affected by the economic slowdown and cuts in public investment and infrastructure. By 2010, approximately half of construction workers were predicted to lose their jobs, while 200,000 workers became unemployed.[39] By 2009, unemployment across all sectors reached 17.5 percent, and 19.5 percent by the end of 2010. Youth unemployment reached even more alarming levels (similar to Greece) – in 2010, 43 percent of young workers did not have a job.[40] Public sector employment reduced by 25 percent; 14,000 public sector jobs were lost (Walter, 2013, p. 189). By 2010, there was a wage cut of around 10 percent in the economy as a whole. The rate was higher – 30 percent – for public employees. The cut for the private sector might indeed have been higher but underreported due to the pervasive informal economy (OECD, 2017).

Despite a very painful economic crisis and the deepest recession in the world during the global financial crisis, we did not observe large-scale labor unrest in Latvia. Rising unemployment and the steep decline in household income did not translate into large-scale strikes, protests, or riots. There were four protests and one riot between 2008 and 2011.[41] The protest in Riga on January 14, 2009, enjoyed large-scale participation (around 10,000 protestors) and later turned into a small-scale riot (there was damage to public and private property, and more than forty people were injured) (BBC News, 2009). On January 27, 2009,

[37] IMF Letter of Intent, 2009. www.imf.org/external/np/loi/2009/lva/072709.pdf. [38] Ibid.
[39] IMF Article IV Consultation, 2010. www.imf.org/external/pubs/ft/scr/2010/cr10356.pdf.
[40] Ibid. [41] A CNTS dataset (2012) recorded one riot and two demonstrations in 2009.

3,700 farmers marched to demand state aid for their sector (Agence France-Presse, 2009). On April 2, 2009, 12,000 public school teachers protested against salary cuts (Associated Press International, 2009). In the largest mobilization, protestors demanded the resignation of the government and an early election; they also expressed outrage about the corruption scandals that had marred the country since early 2007.[42] Hanspeter Kriesi (2012) argues that protests in Latvia became mixed with anti-government and anti-corruption protests, whereas economic policies under external creditors started the mobilizations in countries like Greece and Portugal. After the January riots, the coalition government became unsustainable and resigned in March 2009. Under the new government, protestors blocked the highway to Riga to protest against vehicle tax on December 1, 2009 (Baltic News Service, 2009). Nevertheless, this event did not turn into consecutive strikes or protests.

Latvia is perhaps an even more astonishing case than Ireland in respect of lack of strong protest against the Troika program, as the main reason for painful labor market measures was to address the financial crisis while keeping the currency peg. In other words, labor groups bore the burden of adjustment in the financial sector. Walter (2016) argues that households' foreign currency-denominated debt compelled them to support the currency peg and acquiesce in income loss. However, since the largest group in society is wage earners who rely on the labor market for their livelihoods, we can expect them to be equally, if not more, sensitive to job and income loss. Labor mobility – the easiness of finding a job with similar benefits and income in the event of job loss – perhaps reduced those uncertainties and risks for labor groups.

Latvia has one of the highest levels of labor market mobility among EU member states. The country had a mobility rate of 0.05 (5 percent of workers moving across sectors), on average, between the years 1970 and 2008,[43] while the EU average was 2.1 percent of the total number of workers. Furthermore, Latvia demonstrates how fast mobile workers can adjust to fluctuations and labor market changes. At the start of the crisis at the end of 2009, employment declined in almost all sectors. In the first quarter of 2010, however, employment started picking up in some sectors compared to others. For example, while construction received a substantial hit and did not revive until 2011, mining and agriculture did not experience significant shocks, absorbing some of the workers who had lost their jobs in other sectors. Similarly, accommodation and food services seemed to grow faster than other sectors, surpassing the precrisis period in 2010. Most service activities continued to be stable in terms of

[42] Freedom House, Freedom in the World Report, 2010. www.refworld.org/docid/4c2aff9dc.html.

[43] Author's own calculations; see Section 4 for the measurement of labor mobility and data sources.

Table 12 Number of employees across sectors in Latvia, monthly data 2009–2010

Sector/year	2009	2010	2011
Agriculture; forestry and fishing	80,046	74,345	78,362
Mining and quarrying	2,989	3,904	2,793
Manufacturing	120,819	113,819	116,982
Utilities	26,048	22,982	19,791
Construction	72,817	58,431	62,245
Wholesale and retail trade; repair of motor vehicles and motorcycles	150,769	137,949	139,337
Transport; storage and communication	101,234	99,537	100,719
Accommodation and food service activities	23,171	26,452	25,790
Financial and insurance activities	19,863	16,594	17,719
Real estate; business and administrative activities	63,358	72,481	75,480
Public administration and defense; compulsory social security	71,023	60,602	61,090
Education	84,112	85,820	91,383
Human health and social work activities	50,697	50,325	53,079
Other services	47,785	39,781	36,180

Source: ILO Employment Statistics. https://bit.ly/3vnTStE.

Note: Number of employees in thousands.

employment and did not experience a significant decline. Table 12 shows the quick pickup or mainly stable employment across most sectors in Latvia.

It is notable that high-skilled and low-skilled groups seemed to be differently affected by the crisis and the changes in the Latvian job market. Highly skilled workers appeared to be largely unaffected by the crisis. Workers in sectors such as financial intermediation and social and health work were able to protect their jobs and their income. In fact, total employment of workers with higher education qualificatiohns increased from 289,000 at the end of 2008 to 295,000 in the first quarter of 2009, despite overall rising unemployment.[44] Low-skilled workers, however, seemed to suffer the most due to the crisis and declining employment opportunities. In the first quarter of 2009, 23,000 workers with basic education or less lost their jobs.[45] This corresponds to a quarter of all persons who became unemployed at the beginning of the crisis.

Low-skilled workers, in particular, seemed to use mobility as a strategy to cope with the crisis. The quarterly data demonstrate that low-skilled workers

[44] ILO statistics on employment. https://bit.ly/3GWSHEi. [45] Ibid.

switched toward less affected low-skilled sectors such as agriculture; mining; community, social, and personal services; and hotels and restaurant services after a brief period of unemployment. Across all those sectors, employment increased despite the crisis and the massive contraction in employment (around 100,000 workers lost their jobs in the first two quarters of 2009) in the third and fourth quarters of 2009.[46] In addition, the government implemented a retraining and upskilling program for the unemployed.[47]

Within mobile markets there are also immobile groups such as public school teachers and farmers. For immobile groups (such as workers in education) in Latvia, employment seemed to remain stable or to grow. While agriculture made up of 7.8 percent of total employment in 2008, it increased to 8.8 percent in 2009. The quarterly data show that employment in agriculture grew from 75,100 to 87,400 workers in the second quarter of 2009.[48] Similarly, education sector employment remained stable: although total employment decreased from 84,100 to 81,200 workers in the education sector, the total share of the sector in the economy increased from 8 percent to 9 percent in 2009 compared to 2008.[49] By contrast, manufacturing witnessed a 3 percent decline in total employment, and the construction sector shrank by 4 percent.[50] Teachers, in particular, are very well-organized in Latvia. They have a large trade union, the Latvian Trade Union of Education and Science Employees (LIZDA), which is a social partner with the government. Farmers are represented in a political party, the Union of Greens and Farmers. Partly confirming resource mobilization theory, this organizational capacity might have helped them to stage protests (Associated Press International, 2009). However, the protests did not spread to other groups perhaps because grievances did not increase to a similar extent for larger groups in other sectors.

Unlike Greece, part-time work did not substantially increase in Latvia. Although there was a temporary increase in part-time work in the first quarter of 2009, the level later decreased.[51] This can be explained by labor mobility. When there are lower levels of mobility, workers become "stuck" in their jobs and often switch from full-time and permanent contracts to part-time and temporary jobs, following flexibility measures in the institutional and legal setting, as we observed in Greece. For immobile workers, then, the risk of losing their jobs

---

46 Ibid.

47 IMF Article IV Consultation, 2010. www.elibrary.imf.org/view/journals/002/2010/356/article-A001-en.xml.

48 Ibid. 49 Ibid. 50 Ibid.

51 In the last quarter of 2008, approximately 74,000 people were employed in part-time jobs. The number increased to approximately 90,000 in the first quarter of 2009 and later declined to 77,000 in the second quarter of the same year. See CSP Labor Force Statistics: www.csp.gov.lv/en/dsa.

increases, and the possibility of finding a new job with similar conditions decreases. In a mobile market, however, it is more common for labor groups to switch between jobs. The IMF's labor market reform prescriptions do not create similar uncertainty. Workers switch toward less affected sectors, join retraining programs, and retain the possibility of finding a job with similar benefits once the economy starts recovering. Low-skilled workers in Latvia did not move to part-time jobs in large numbers after the flexibility measures were introduced. Instead, they either became unemployed (with the possibility of returning to the market following the recovery) or moved to sectors such as agriculture, mining, community and health services, and hotel and restaurant services. In lowering the risks associated with unemployment, of course, Latvia's generous unemployment replacement rate (82 percent of one's salary in 2009 and 85 percent in 2010) might also have played a role.[52] Workers had a viable fallback option. However, these benefits last for a maximum of eight months and are not a sustainable option without a job with similar pay and benefits in the near future.[53]

The critical difference determining how mobile and immobile job markets are differently affected by labor market deregulation conditionality is level and type of risk. In an immobile market, there are very high levels of uncertainty with respect to keeping a job, the benefits associated with it, and future income; whereas, in a mobile market, switching jobs does not necessarily bring increased risks. In the latter case, labor market changes do not lead to a sudden outburst of unrest. Similarly, if there were not many labor conditions, risks would not increase to a similar extent, as demonstrated by the case of Portugal.

5.4 Portugal in 2011: Responsiveness of an Immobile Market to Labor Conditions

Portugal signed a trilateral agreement with the IMF, European Commission, and the ECB in May 2011. The country received 26 billion euros from the IMF under its EFF arrangement and 52 billion euros from the European partners and the ECB over three years.[54]

The Portuguese government initially responded to the global financial crisis with expansionary policies and implemented a fiscal stimulus package in 2008 and 2009 (Silva, 2022). Nevertheless, in mid-2010, the budget deficit started to rise, and sovereign yields almost peaked at 1,500 basis points.[55] The budgetary

[52] OECD. Net Replacement Rate in Unemployment. https://stats.oecd.org/Index.aspx?DataSetCode=NRR.

[53] State Social Insurance Agency of the Republic of Latvia. https://bit.ly/48dGsP2.

[54] IMF Letter of Intent, 2011. www.imf.org/external/np/loi/2011/prt/051711.pdf.

[55] IMF Article IV Consultation and Sixth Review under the Extended Arrangement, 2012. www.imf.org/external/pubs/ft/scr/2013/cr1318.pdf.

proposal of the minority socialist government under José Sócrates to address the crisis without an external bailout was defeated in parliament in March 2011. Sócrates then resigned and called for early elections in June. During the same period, the prime minister also asked for help from the Troika; the Memorandum of Understanding was negotiated and signed in May 2011 (Moury and Standring, 2017).

The macroeconomic crisis in Portugal was very similar to the crisis in Greece in 2010 in terms of fiscal imbalances underlying the governmental budget, the sudden decline of foreign capital inflow, the failed attempt at recovery through fiscal stimulus, and structural weaknesses in the economy. Both countries had domestic demand-driven growth in the 2000s and ran very high levels of current account deficits before the crisis. And, they financed the gap by borrowing from the international markets (Dooley, 2018). With the start of the global financial crisis, such inflows stopped and current account balances deteriorated further. The budgetary deficit reached 14 percent of Greece's GDP in 2008, while it was 12 percent for Portugal in the same year.[56]

Both Greece and Portugal became members of the European Economic Community (ECC) after a period of dictatorships; the authoritarian regime fell in Greece in 1977 and in Portugal in 1974. Rapid democratization largely coincided with rapid deregulation, privatization, and economic growth, in part thanks to funds from the ECC (Dooley, 2018), Both economies largely became uncompetitive in export markets in the 2000s, switched their economic production toward nontradable sectors, and had a domestic demand-led growth (Magone, 2014). While the drying up of international credit and capital inflows resulted in problems in the financial sectors in both Ireland and Latvia, the Great Recession exposed underlying problems in the political economies of Greece and Portugal that had existed for some time.

Finally, the labor market in Portugal is highly dualized, as it is in Greece. While workers in the large public sector and large private enterprises enjoyed higher wages and greater employment protection against firing, collective dismissals, and temporary and fixed-term contracts, such protection is almost absent in parts of the private sector, especially in smaller and medium-sized businesses (Lopes, 2003; Papapetrou, 2006; Magone, 2014, p. 349; Christopoulou and Monastiriotis, 2016). Dualization makes the potential loss of benefits as a result of flexibilization measures even more significant for workers in Greece and Portugal.

[56] World Bank. Current Account Balance (% of GDP). https://data.worldbank.org/indicator/BN.CAB.XOKA.GD.ZS?end=2021&start=2021&view=bar.

Table 13 Number of employees across sectors in Portugal, annual data 2011–2013

Sector/year	2011	2012	2013
Agriculture; forestry and fishing	485,781	493,595	455,634
Mining and quarrying	18,447	13,772	13,253
Manufacturing	786,161	744,015	708,903
Utilities	48,431	46,252	43,428
Construction	424,726	344,584	289,945
Wholesale and retail trade; repair of motor vehicles and motorcycles	695,437	662,855	647,582
Transport; storage and communication	250,329	251,014	270,720
Accommodation and food service activities	287,551	278,042	290,663
Financial and insurance activities	104,136	97,378	87,122
Real estate; business and administrative activities	337,182	322,697	338,607
Public administration and defence; compulsory social security	307,406	290,846	293,836
Education	365,123	370,262	357,373
Human health and social work activities	363,528	372,284	371,062
Other services	283,863	279,634	285,983

Source: ILO Employment Statistics. https://ilostat.ilo.org/.

Note: Numbers of employees in thousands.

Portugal is also very similar to Greece in terms of low levels of labor market mobility. The cross-sectoral mobility level was 0.002 (0.2 percent) in Portugal in 2011 when the country borrowed from the IMF and 0.003 (0.3 percent) the following year, compared to 5 percent in 2008 and 1 percent in 2011 in Latvia. In terms of average job tenure, Greece and Portugal had higher average job tenure (approximately 12.4 years) at the start of their IMF programs, compared to Ireland in 2010 (9.8 years) and Latvia in 2009 (7.9 years). To be sure, employment did not drastically decline in Portugal to the same degree that it did in Greece, partly because there were fewer flexibilization measures that made hiring and firing easier and encouraged fixed-term contracts. Table 13 depicts changes in the number of workers employed across different sectors between 2011 and 2013.

Table 13 shows that employment declined in most sectors in Portugal, but this decline was not as drastic as that experienced in Greece. Furthermore, there was even a modest increase in some sectors such as transportation and storage and accommodation and food service activities. The sectors did not peak to the extent that they did in Latvia, but we can see some modest levels of mobility.

Second, deregulation of the dualized labor market under the Troika program was not as strong and as sharp as it was in Greece. For example, the percentage of workers represented in collective bargaining agreements did not fall as much in Portugal as it did in Greece. Collective bargaining coverage remained steady at around 76 percent of eligible workers (78.1 percent in 2011, 75.5 percent in 2012, and 76.5 percent in 2013) as opposed to a 62.7 percent decline in Greece between 2010 and 2013.[57] Finally, wages in Portugal did not collapse as they did in Greece (see Figure 9). There was even an increase in 2014, with the reduction in labor tax, though wages fell back to 2013 levels in 2015. The pacing of labor conditions in Portugal and the fact that they were not as extensive as in Greece prevented a sudden loss of income and rights and the rise of risks and uncertainties.

Although we did not observe large-scale unrest in Portugal such as we saw in Greece, we did see very high levels of responsiveness to any labor market changes and deregulation in the country. In fact, it is very interesting to note how the protests almost perfectly synchronized with the proposed labor market changes in the IMF programs, almost month by month. The Portuguese case shows that in an immobile labor market, labor groups respond to proposed labor market reforms with an almost immediate reaction.

For example, in the first Letter of Intent in May 2011, the program included reductions in severance payments in job contracts as a structural benchmark. However, it also envisaged cuts in labor taxes to increase competitiveness.[58] The cuts indirectly benefited labor groups. Even though there were protests against austerity under José Sócrates' socialist government in March 2011, we did not see an upsurge in protests following the program. The first review and the Letter of Intent in September 2011, however, introduced privatization measures for the state-owned enterprises.[59] On October 15, 2011, immediately following the review, 20,000 people rallied against the program in Lisbon. In Oporto, another 20,000 were estimated to have joined their counterparts in the capital city (Agence France-Presse, 2011). The protestors' targets were the government and the IMF: protest banners read "IMF, get out of here" (Agence France-Presse, 2011) and the protestors chanted "Out, out of here, hunger, misery and the IMF" (Silva, 2022). On November 24, 2011, there was a general strike organized by the General Confederation of Portuguese Workers

[57] OECD. Collective Bargaining Coverage Data. https://stats.oecd.org/index.aspx?DataSetCode =CBC.

[58] IMF Letter of Intent, Memorandum of Economic and Financial Policies, and Technical Memorandum of Understanding, May 2011. www.imf.org/external/np/loi/2011/prt/051711.pdf.

[59] IMF Letter of Intent, Memorandum of Economic and Financial Policies, and Technical Memorandum of Understanding, September 2011. www.imf.org/~/media/external/np/loi/2011/prt/090111.ashx.

(Confederação Geral dos Trabalhadores Portugueses, CGTP) and the General Union of Workers (União Geral de Trabalhadores, UGT) to protest the measures (Silva, 2022). The second review in December 2011 did not introduce any new labor conditions. The program was peacefully implemented during this period without any large-scale protests or demonstrations.

The initial round of protests intensified in the second half of 2012, in parallel with the increasing labor market deregulation proposals of the Troika program for Portugal. The sixth review set a structural benchmark for decentralization of collective agreements in September 2012. In particular, the new Prime Minister, Pedro Passos Coelho, announced that workers' social security contributions might increase from 11 to 18 percent of their wages. The protests were commensurate with the initial anti-austerity demonstrations in September 2011 (New York Times, 2012). The biggest protest, with the participation of approximately 500,000 in Lisbon and around one million in total around the country, was organized on September 15, 2012. The protest was called "To hell with Troika! we want our lives" (Silva, 2022, p. 104).

In fact, the third year of the program (2013) had the highest number of policy prescriptions related to the labor market and was the most intense year in terms of labor unrest in Portugal. Specifically, five structural benchmarks were identified in the program.[60] First, the program envisaged reorganizing employment conditions such as work hours, holidays, and firing costs in the civil service in accordance with private sector employment. Second, the government was asked to combine the public sector workers' pension fund with the general pension scheme. Third, the statutory retirement age was set to be increased to sixty-six. Fourth, severance compensation for new permanent contracts was decreased in labor laws. Finally, the mobility pool – in which redundant civil servants are kept in the registry and then allocated to appropriate jobs – was set to be reduced. Before the formal announcement of the program, protestors marched again against the government and the trilateral agreement on March 3, 2013 (DW.com, 2013). Reportedly, around 200,000 protestors gathered in front of the Ministry of Finance to protest the Troika measures (DW.com, 2013). On June 27, 2013, immediately after the review and the conditions became public, transport workers announced a general strike, freezing the country's bus, metro, and train services (Reuters, 2013). Carlos Silva, leader of the second biggest trade union, UGT, argued after the June strike that "austerity policies punish the country,

[60] IMF Letter of Intent, Memorandum of Economic and Financial Policies, and Technical Memorandum of Understanding, October 2013. www.imf.org/external/np/loi/2013/prt/102413.pdf.

violate the people, and penalize workers and pensioners, so the strike will be a cry of resistance to these policies" (Reuters, 2013).

The mobilization in Portugal was particularly surprising given its historical context. The scholarship has often underlined the relative acquiescence in Portugal as opposed to a protest culture and mobilization. In fact, the general strike jointly called by two unions was the first in twenty-two years (Silva, 2022). As Accornero and Ramos Pinto (2015) remark, although "old" actors such as trade unions and leftist political parties and movements took a leading role, mobilization spread throughout society beyond the traditional constituencies of these actors. Traditional representatives of labor interests were joined by "new" movements and society at large against labor market reform measures. Furthermore, these actors found it hard to mobilize groups when there were not any labor market deregulation measures. In the period between December 2011 and the second half of 2012, structural adjustment programs did not include any labor market measures. "Despite the union organisation, attendance at the demonstration in the capital did not exceed 1000 people" (Silva, 2022, p. 104) in the protest on May 12, 2012.

The Portuguese case demonstrates the receptivity of an immobile market to labor conditionality. It shows that decentralization measures and those that reduce the costs of hiring and firing in a dualized labor market might generate uncertainty and loss of income for insider workers in an immobile market. Reuters anecdotally reports that despite high taxes and anti-austerity sentiments, retaining jobs was the priority for Portuguese workers. It cites an electrician, who says: "It's simple – if I don't work, I don't eat. The government disgusts me, the austerity is stifling us, but protesting won't feed my family" (Reuters, 2013).

6 Conclusion

In this Element, I analyzed the impact of labor market mobility (the ease of changing jobs and sectors) and the IMF's labor market reforms on labor unrest (i.e. protests, strikes, and riots related to labor issues). The study shows that IMF-sponsored labor market reforms implemented in an immobile labor market lead to an increase in the likelihood of labor unrest. The IMF's labor reforms both heighten the risks that immobile workers are exposed to and cause them to lose real and prospective benefits and income. As a result, they react against programs to block their implementation. Statistical analysis of a global sample of IMF program countries supports this thesis as well as individual-level data that demonstrate the vulnerability of immobile groups to unemployment and economic hardship. I also demonstrated how labor conditions and mobility interact by looking at European borrowers of the Fund following the 2008 financial crisis: namely, Greece (a case of low labor mobility and a high number of labor reforms with a high level of labor unrest), Ireland (a case of high labor mobility and a low number of reforms with minimal to no unrest), Latvia (a high number of labor reforms in a highly mobile labor market, and therefore moderate to low levels of unrest), and Portugal (low labor mobility, yet fewer labor market reforms and hence moderate levels of unrest).

The Element offers several contributions to the literature on the impact of IMF programs on political and labor mobilization. In previous studies, scholars have demonstrated that programs increase the likelihood of human rights violations and governmental instability due to the formation and mobilization of opposition. This Element aims to shed light on the causes underlying the compounded economic hardship for some labor groups, and hence their opposition to and mobilization against programs. It argues that labor market reforms implemented under IMF programs challenge the interests of immobile labor groups. In an immobile labor market, labor is not as flexible and so is less able to adjust to the flexibilization measures brought by an IMF program. Even when workers adjust, they lose in real terms such as in income and rights. In other words, the study explains the link between IMF programs and rising economic hardship and grievances, and how these turn into unrest. Second, this Element is one of the first studies in the literature that elaborates on the importance of intersectoral labor market mobility in shaping domestic preferences and reactions against programs. The impact of labor market mobility on trade politics is well-known in the literature. This study offers an original contribution by discussing its consequences in terms of the impact of an international actor, the IMF, on labor mobilizations. Furthermore, it expands the theory of factor mobility (mobility between land, labor, and capital) and interindustry mobility (mobility across manufacturing sectors) to intersectoral labor mobility (movement across sectors) and looks at how and when wage differentials across sectors are low enough to allow labor to move to an alternative sector of employment. It suggests that the possibility of moving to a new job if one's sector takes a hit provides insurance and reduces the negative impact of labor market flexibilization measures. Hence, the Element analyzes the mitigating role of smooth movement on workers' welfare in a broader sense across all sectors of the economy.

The study is, of course, not without its limitations. Protest and strike data are notoriously difficult to gather and are often incomplete (Abouharb and Cingranelli, 2007; Beissinger et al., 2014). Similarly, employment data for some observations is based on ILO projections, especially for less developed countries. Future studies building on this study could aim to gather more complete survey data with workers from different sectors and how, and when, they switch sectors. Naturally, in this study, the emphasis has been on the lack of labor mobility in explaining unrest. Future studies could complete this picture by looking more closely at cases of labor mobility.

Scholars could, in the future, also extend the theory of cross-sectoral mobility to study support for trade and globalization. For example, the process of globalization might create deeper economic hardship for immobile labor groups and hence they might be more likely to oppose globalization, paving the way for a backlash against globalization. This might translate into populist votes, for instance. Scholars could also widen the theory and apply it to other topics that are related to labor market risks and uncertainties, such as attitudes toward immigration, climate change, and foreign direct investment. This might have implications in terms of voting behavior and who votes for parties that run on certain platforms. Scholars of labor market reform could look at how (im)mobile markets are affected by large-scale reform initiatives, not only under IMF programs but other international organizations as well as by domestic governments. The literature is in huge need of studies that investigate the causes of mobility based on political factors such as social policy preferences and the historical evolution of labor markets, complementing studies in the field of economics.

Finally, the analysis in this Element offers a possible and immediate policy lesson in the design of IMF programs. In prospective programs, Fund officials might pay closer attention to labor mobility levels. Program implementation might be paced. Initial fiscal adjustment measures might be used to create space for expenditure in the budget, as in the case of Portugal in 2011, and immobile sectors might be compensated via upskilling and training programs, as in Latvia in 2008. The Fund and governments could think more carefully about the reintegration into the labor market of immobile workers who became unemployed. Then, these programs might ultimately have fewer human costs for labor groups.

Appendix I: Sectors Used in the Calculation of Intersectoral Mobility

ILO Cross-Sectoral (ISIC 4) (ILOSTAT)

A	Agriculture; Forestry and fishing
B	Mining and quarrying
C	Manufacturing
D	Electricity; Gas, steam and air conditioning supply
E	Water supply; Sewerage, waste management and remediation activities
F	Construction
G	Wholesale and retail trade; Repair of motor vehicles, motorcycles
H	Transportation and storage
I	Accommodation and food service activities
J	Information and communication
K	Financial and insurance activities
L	Real estate activities
M	Professional, scientific and technical activities
N	Administrative and support service activities
O	Public administration and defense; Compulsory social security
P	Education
Q	Human health and social work activities
R	Arts, entertainment and recreation
S	Other service activities
T	Activities of households as employers; Undifferentiated goods and services-producing activities of households for own use
X	Not elsewhere classified

Appendix II: Labor Conditions in Greece (2010), Latvia (2008), and Portugal (2011)

Labor Conditions in Greece (May 2010 Letter of Intent)

- Reduce public wage bill by cutting bonuses/allowances and pension bonuses (except minimum pensions). (Prior action)
- Adopt a comprehensive pension reform that reduces the projected increase in public spending on pensions over the period 2010–60 to 2.5 percent of GDP. (Structural benchmark)
- Prepare a privatization plan for the divestment of state assets and enterprises with the aim of raising at least one billion euro a year during the period 2011–13. (Structural benchmark)
- Following consultation with thirty-seven social partners and within the framework of EU law, the government will reform the legal framework for wage bargaining in the private sector, including by eliminating asymmetry in arbitration. (Soft condition)
- The government will adopt legislation for minimum entry-level wages in order to promote employment creation for groups at risk such as the young and long-term unemployed. (Soft condition)
- In parallel, the government will implement the new control system for undeclared work and modernize labor market institutions. (Soft condition)
- Employment protection legislation will be revised, including provisions to extend probationary periods, recalibrate rules governing collective dismissals, and facilitate greater use of part-time work. (Soft condition)

Labor Conditions in Latvia (2009 Letter of Intent)

- An indicative ceiling on the general government wage bill. (Quantitative indicative target)
- National Tripartite Co-operation Council to establish a Committee to Promote Wage Restraint. (Structural benchmark)
- Wages: prepare a comprehensive report on proposed revisions to the public sector wage grid and relative wage adjustment across public institutions. (Structural benchmark)
- Put in place a wage-setting mechanism in line with the fixed exchange-rate regime. (Soft condition)
- Index pensions only to inflation. (Soft condition)

Labor Conditions in Portugal (2011 Letter of Intent)

- Submit to parliament a law, already agreed with social partners, to align and reduce severance payments in all new contracts (fixed-term and open-ended). (Structural benchmark)
- Finalize calibration of fiscal reform to reduce unit labor costs via a deficit-neutral reduction in labor taxes. (Structural benchmark)

Appendix III: List of Interviews

Interview No.	Interviewee name or affiliation	Interview date	Interview location
Interview No. 1	George Argeitis, Scientific Director of GSEE	September 25, 2014	Athens, Greece
Interview No. 2	Louka Katseli, Minister of Economy and Minister of Labor and Social Protection (2009–11)	September 24, 2014	Athens, Greece
Interview No. 3	George Papaconstantinou, Minister of Finance (2009–12)	October 1, 2014	Athens, Greece
Interview No. 4	Adam Bennett, Deputy Director of European Department of the IMF (2009–11)	October 25, 2014	Oxford, UK
Interview No. 5	Senior European Commission official	November 6, 2014	Brussels, Belgium
Interview No. 6	Senior European Commission official	November 7, 2014	Brussels, Belgium
Interview No. 7	Senior IMF official in IMF EU Office	January 26, 2014	Brussels, Belgium
Interview No. 8	Senior IMF official	July 13, 2021	Online

Appendix IV: Descriptive Statistics

Variables	(1) N	(2) mean	(3) sd	(4) min	(5) max
IMF program participation	7,115	0.299	0.458	0	1
Labor conditions (count)	6,486	0.306	1.166	0	13
High labor conditions	6,486	0.0219	0.146	0	1
Protest	4,114	0.144	0.627	0	11
Strike	4,110	0.395	1.885	0	65
Riot	4,113	0.0477	0.318	0	9
Unrest	4,110	0.583	2.340	0	75
Mobility score	5,075	0.0158	0.0209	0	0.174
Strike event	3,836	0.276	1.373	0	28
Strikes (CNTS)	8,961	0.116	0.509	0	13
Riots (CNTS)	8,960	0.417	1.716	0	55
Demonstrations (CNTS)	8,960	0.461	1.655	0	60
Unrest (CNTS)	8,957	0.995	3.225	0	85
Relative freq. of labor conditions	1,748	0.0287	0.0515	0	0.500
Weighted labor conditions	6,486	0.421	1.704	0	26
Urban population (% pop.)	3,672	45.97	22.98	4.080	100
Population (logged)	3,646	15.85	1.525	12.26	20.99
External debt (% GNI)	4,744	1.162e + 14	2.102e + 14	1.295e + 08	9.956e + 14
GDP per capita	5,454	9,711	15,248	4	141,635
GDP per capita growth	5,454	14,339	18,245	285.6	154,096
Democracy	7,375	11.37	7.303	0	20
Recidivism	4,190	1.433	1.887	0	5
Current account (% GDP)	4,615	-2.71e-09	5.97e-08	-1.85e-06	8.82e-07

Appendix V: Additional Robustness Checks

Variables	Strike events	Unrest	Strikes (CNTS)
Mobility score	-5.014	-3.035	-2.669
	(4.826)	(5.563)	(5.559)
Labor conditions	0.0307	0.0649	0.0119
	(0.0521)	(0.0541)	(0.0727)
Mobility score x	-2.960	-1.551	-3.562
labor conditions	(2.467)	(2.197)	(3.753)
Democracy	0.0375	0.0985***	0.115***
	(0.0304)	(0.0267)	(0.0333)
Urban population	0.0181	0.000474	0.0125
(% pop.)	(0.0121)	(0.00836)	(0.0134)
GDP per capita	1.57e-05	3.33e-05	4.79e-05
(lagged)	(2.51e-05)	(2.89e-05)	(4.11e-05)
Population	0.613***	0.516***	0.325**
(logged)	(0.127)	(0.0875)	(0.134)
GDP per capita	4.05e-05	0.000129***	-0.000131
growth (lagged)	(7.39e-05)	(4.84e-05)	(9.34e-05)
Constant	-11.12***	-12.23***	-6.249**
	(2.190)	(1.537)	(2.637)
Observations	847	847	844
Number of countries	94	94	94

Note: Negative binomial regression for panel data; Standard errors in parentheses. *** p <0.01, ** p <0.05, * p <0.1.

References

Abouharb, M. R. and Cingranelli, D. (2007) *Human Rights and Structural Adjustment*. Cambridge: Cambridge University Press.

Abouharb, M. R. and Cingranelli, D. L. (2009) "IMF Programs and Human Rights, 1981–2003," *Review of International Organizations*, 4(1), pp. 47–72.

Accornero, G. and Ramos Pinto, P. (2015) "'Mild Mannered'? Protest and Mobilisation in Portugal under Austerity, 2010–2013," *West European Politics*, 38(3), pp. 491–515.

Agence France-Presse (2009) "Farmers in Recession-Hit Latvia Protest for State Aid," January 27.

Agence France-Presse (2011) "Tens of Thousands Protest Austerity Policies in Portugal," October 15.

Andritzky, J., Andritzky, M. J. R., Munkacsi, Z., and Wang, K. (2021) *How to Gain the Most from Structural Conditionality of IMF-Supported Programs*. International Monetary Fund.

Andronikidou, A. and Kovras, I. (2012) "Cultures of Rioting and Anti-Systemic Politics in Southern Europe," *West European Politics*, 35(4), pp. 707–725.

Aslanidis, P. (2016) "Populist Social Movements of the Great Recession," *Mobilization: An International Quarterly*, 21(3), pp. 301–321.

Associated Press International (2009) "Thousands of Teachers in Latvia Protest Wage Cuts," April 2.

Baltic News Service (2009) "People in Eastern Latvia Block Highway to Protest Increase of Annual Vehicle Tax," December 1.

Ban, C. and Gallagher, K. (2015) "Recalibrating Policy Orthodoxy: The IMF since the Great Recession: IMF, Great Recession, Policy Change," *Governance*, 28(2), pp. 131–146.

Banks, A. S. (2008) "Cross-National Time-Series Data Archive (CNTS) 1815–2007," Harvard Dataverse, V1. https://doi.org/10.7910/DVN/EARQIG.

Bas, M. A. and Stone, R. W. (2014) "Adverse Selection and Growth under IMF Programs," *Review of International Organizations*, 9(1), pp. 1–28.

BBC News (2009) "Anti-Government Rioting Hits Riga," January 14.http://news.bbc.co.uk/2/hi/europe/7827708.stm.

Beissinger, M., Sasse, G., and Straif, K. (2014) "'An End to Patience?' The Great Recession and Economic Protest in Eastern Europe," in Bartels, L. M. and Bermeo, N. (eds.) *Mass Politics in Tough Times: Opinions, Votes and Protest in the Great Recession*. Oxford: Oxford University Press, pp. 334–371.

Bērziņš, J. (2014) "Ignacio Rangel Visits Latvia: Crisis and the Political Economy of Duality," *Debatte: Journal of Contemporary Central and Eastern Europe*, 22(1), pp. 81–102.

Bienen, H. S. and Gersovitz, M. (1985) "Economic Stabilization, Conditionality, and Political Stability," *International Organization*, 39(4), pp. 729–754.

Blanchard, O. and Wolfers, J. (2000) "The Role of Shocks and Institutions in the Rise of European Unemployment: The Aggregate Evidence," *Economic Journal*, 110(462), pp. C1–C33.

Blanchard, O. J., Jaumotte, F., and Loungani, P. (2014) "Labor Market Policies and IMF Advice in Advanced Economies during the Great Recession," *IZA Journal of Labor Policy*, 3(1), pp. 1–23.

Burns, J. (2010) "Demonstrators in Ireland Protest Austerity Plan," November 27. www.nytimes.com/2010/11/28/world/europe/28dublin.html.

Cameron, A. C. and Trivedi, P. K. (2013) *Regression Analysis of Count Data* (Vol. 53). Cambridge: Cambridge university press.

Cannon, B. and Murphy, M. P. (2015) "Where Are the Pots and Pans? Collective Responses in Ireland to Neoliberalization in a Time of Crisis: Learning from Latin America," *Irish Political Studies*, 30(1), pp. 1–19.

Caraway, T. (2006) "Freedom of Association: Battering Ram or Trojan Horse?," *Review of International Political Economy*, 13(2), pp. 210–232.

Caraway, T. L., Rickard, S. J., and Anner, M. S. (2012) "International Negotiations and Domestic Politics: The Case of IMF Labor Market Conditionality," *International Organization*, 66(1), pp. 27–61.

Casper, B. A. (2017) "IMF Programs and the Risk of a Coup d'état," *Journal of Conflict Resolution*, 61(5), pp. 964–996.

Chapman, T., Fang, S., LI, X, and Stone, R. W. (2017) "Mixed Signals: IMF Lending and Capital Markets," *British Journal of Political Science*, 47(2), pp. 329–349.

Christopoulou, R. and Monastiriotis, V. (2016) "Public–Private Wage Duality during the Greek Crisis," *Oxford Economic Papers*, 68(1), pp. 174–196.

Chwieroth, J. M. (2007) "Testing and Measuring the Role of Ideas: The Case of Neoliberalism in the International Monetary Fund," *International Studies Quarterly*, 51(1), pp. 5–30.

Chwieroth, J. M. (2014) "Controlling Capital: The International Monetary Fund and Transformative Incremental Change from within International Organisations," *New Political Economy*, 19(3), pp. 445–469.

Chwieroth, J. M. (2015) "Professional Ties That Bind: How Normative Orientations Shape IMF Conditionality," *Review of International Political Economy*, 22(4), pp. 757–787.

Copelovitch, M. S. (2010) "Master or Servant? Common Agency and the Political Economy of IMF Lending," *International Studies Quarterly*, 54(1), pp. 49–77.

Copelovitch, M., Frieden, J., and Walter, S. (2016) "The Political Economy of the Euro Crisis," *Comparative Political Studies*, 49(7), pp. 811–840.

Culpepper, P. D. and Regan, A. (2014) "Why Don't Governments Need Trade Unions Anymore? The Death of Social Pacts in Ireland and Italy," *Socio-Economic Review*, 12(4), pp. 723–745.

Dahl, R. A. (2020). *On Democracy*. E-book. Yale University Press. https://yalebooks.co.uk/book/9780300257991/on-democracy/.

Dang, T. A. and Stone, R. W. (2021) "Multinational Banks and IMF Conditionality," *International Studies Quarterly*, 65(2), pp. 375–386.

Dedoussopoulos, A., Aranitou, V., Koutentakis, F., and Maropoulou, M. (2013) "Assessing the Impact of the Memoranda on Greek Labour Market and Labour Relations," International Labour Organization Working Paper, No. 53.

Donadio, R. and Kitsantonis, N. (2011) "Thousands Protest Austerity Bill in Greece," October 19. www.nytimes.com/2011/10/20/world/europe/greek-workers-start-two-day-anti-austerity-strike.html.

Dooley, N. (2018) "Portugal's Economic Crisis: Overheating without Accelerating," in Parker, O. and Tsarouhas, D. (eds.) *Crisis in the Eurozone Periphery*. Cham: Springer International Publishing, pp. 73–91.

Doyle, D. (2010) "Politics and Privatization: Exogenous Pressures, Domestic Incentives and State Divestiture in Latin America," *Journal of Public Policy*, 30(3), pp. 291–320.

Dreher, A. (2006) "IMF and Economic Growth: The Effects of Programs, Loans, and Compliance with Conditionality," *World Development*, 34(5), pp. 769–788. https://doi.org/10.1016/j.worlddev.2005.11.002.

Dreher, A. and Gassebner, M. (2012) "Do IMF and World Bank Programs Induce Government Crises? An Empirical Analysis," *International Organization*, 66(2), pp. 329–358.

Dreher, A. and Jensen, N. M. (2007) "Independent Actor or Agent? An Empirical Analysis of the Impact of U.S. Interests on International Monetary Fund Conditions," *Journal of Law and Economics*, 50(1), pp. 105–124.

Dreher, A. and Vaubel, R. (2004) "The Causes and Consequences of IMF Conditionality," *Emerging Markets Finance and Trade*, 40(3), pp. 26–54.

Dreher, A., Sturm, J.-E., and Vreeland, J. R. (2015) "Politics and IMF Conditionality," *Journal of Conflict Resolution*, 59(1), pp. 120–148.

DW.com (2013) "Portugal Protests Austerity," March 3. www.dw.com/en/portugal-protesters-march-against-austerity/a-16642036.

Estevez-Abe, M., Iversen, T., and Soskice, D. (2001) "Social Protection and the Formation of Skills: A Reinterpretation of the Welfare State," in Hall, P. A. and Soskice, D. (eds.) *Varieties of Capitalism*. 1st ed. Oxford: Oxford University Press, pp. 145–183.

European Commission Directorate-General for Economic and Financial Affairs (2010) "The Economic Adjustment Programme for Greece," Occasional Papers No. 61. https://ec.europa.eu/economy_finance/publications/occasional_paper/2010/pdf/ocp61_en.pdf.

Fearon, J. D. and Laitin, D. D. (2003) "Ethnicity, Insurgency, and Civil War," *American Political Science Review*, 97(1), pp. 75–90.

Feldmann, M. (2000) "Understanding the Baltic and Estonian Puzzles: The Political Economy of Rapid External Liberalization in Estonia and Latvia." Bank of Finland Institute for Economies in Transition (BOFIT), No. 11.

Franklin, J. (1997) "IMF Conditionality, Threat Perception, and Political Repression: A Cross-National Analysis," *Comparative Political Studies*, 30(5), pp. 576–606.

Franzosi, R. (1995) *The Puzzle of Strikes: Class and State Strategies in Postwar Italy*. Cambridge: Cambridge University Press.

Frieden, J. A. (1991) "Invested Interests: The Politics of National Economic Policies in a World of Global Finance," *International Organization*, 45(4), pp. 425–451.

Fuller, G. and Jones, E. (2014) "Europe and the Global Economic Crisis," in Tiersky, R. and Jones, E. (eds.) *Europe Today: A twenty-First Century Introduction*. New York: Rowman & Littlefield, pp 343–365.

Gartzke, E. and Naoi, M. (2011) "Multilateralism and Democracy: A Dissent regarding Keohane, Macedo, and Moravcsik," *International Organization*, 65(3), pp. 589–598.

Garuda, G. (2000) "The Distributional Effects of IMF Programs: A Cross-Country Analysis," *World Development*, 28(6), pp. 1031–1051.

Gould, E. R. (2003) "Money Talks: Supplementary Financiers and International Monetary Fund Conditionality," *International Organization*, 57(3), pp. 551–586.

GSEE (2010) "Call for 24-Hour General Strike," Press Release, April 27. https://gsee.gr/?p=3211.

Gurr, T. R. (2015) *Why Men Rebel*. New York: Routledge.

Hall, P. A. and Gingerich, D. W. (2009) "Varieties of Capitalism and Institutional Complementarities in the Political Economy: An Empirical Analysis," *British Journal of Political Science*, 39(3), pp. 449–482.

Hall, P. A. and Soskice, D. (2001) "An Introduction to Varieties of Capitalism," in Hall, P. A and Soskice D. (eds.) *Varieties of Capitalism: The Institutional Foundations of Comparative Advantage*. Oxford: Oxford University Press, pp. 1–68.

Hall, P. A. and Thelen, K. (2008) "Institutional Change in Varieties of Capitalism," *Socio-Economic Review*, 7(1), pp. 7–34.

Hardiman, N. (1988) *Pay, Politics, and Economic Performance in Ireland, 1970–1987*. Oxford: Oxford University Press.

Hardiman, N. and Metinsoy, S. (2019) "Power, Ideas, and National Preferences: Ireland and the FTT," *Journal of European Public Policy*, 26(11), pp. 1600–1619.

Hardiman, N., Spanou, C., Araújo, J. F., and MacCarthaigh, M. (2019) "Tangling with the Troika: 'Domestic Ownership' as Political and Administrative Engagement in Greece, Ireland, and Portugal," *Public Management Review*, 21(9), pp. 1265–1286.

Hartzell, C. A., Hoddie, M., and Bauer, M. (2010) "Economic Liberalization via IMF Structural Adjustment: Sowing the Seeds of Civil War?," *International Organization*, 64(2), pp. 339–356.

Hegre, H. (2001) "Toward a Democratic Civil Peace? Democracy, Political Change, and Civil War, 1816–1992," *American Political Science Review*, 95(1), pp. 33–48.

Hiscox, M. J. (2001) "Class versus Industry Cleavages: Inter-Industry Factor Mobility and the Politics of Trade," *International Organization*, 55(1), pp. 1–46.

Hiscox, M. J. (2002) "Commerce, Coalitions, and Factor Mobility: Evidence from Congressional Votes on Trade Legislation," *American Political Science Review*, 96(3), pp. 593–608.

Hiscox, M. J. (2020) *International Trade and Political Conflict*. Princeton, NJ: Princeton University Press.

Hiscox, M. J. and Rickard, S. J. (2002) "'Birds of a Different Feather?': Varieties of Capitalism, Factor Specificity, and Interindustry Labor Movements," Working Paper, Harvard University.

Hünermund, P. and Louw, B. (2020) "On the Nuisance of Control Variables in Regression Analysis," arXiv Preprint, arXiv: 2005.10314.

ICTU (2011) "Growth Is the Key: Pre-Budget Submission." https://bit.ly/48fVkwu.

ICTU (2013) "Congress Confirms Feb 9 'Lift the Burden' Protests Will Go Ahead," February 7. https://ictu.ie/news/congress-confirms-feb-9-lift-burden-protests-will-go-ahead.

IMF (2010) "IMF Executive Board Approves €22.5 Billion Extended Arrangement for Ireland," Press Release, December 16. www.imf.org/en/News/Articles/2015/09/14/01/49/pr10496.

IMF News (2011) "IMF Survey: Greece: Reform Agenda Essential for Growth," July 15. www.imf.org/external/pubs/ft/survey/so/2011/car071511a.htm.

Irish Examiner (2010) "TUI Members Vote to Suspend Industrial Action," November 5. www.irishexaminer.com/news/arid-30480641.html.

Irish Times (2009) "Unions Announce Second Day of Strikes for Next Week," November 24. www.irishtimes.com/news/unions-announce-second-day-of-strikes-for-next-week-1.849581.

Iversen, T. and Soskice, D. (2001) "An Asset Theory of Social Policy Preferences," *American Political Science Review*, 95(4), pp. 875–893.

Kalyvas, S. N. and Marantzidis, N. (2002) "Greek Communism, 1968–2001," *East European Politics and Societies*, 16(3), pp. 665–690.

Karyotis, G. and Rüdig, W. (2018) "The Three Waves of Anti-Austerity Protest in Greece, 2010–2015," *Political Studies Review*, 16(2), pp. 158–169.

Katsoridas, D. and Lambousaki, S. (2013) "Το απεργιακό φαινόμενο στην Ελλάδα κατά το 2012" ["The Strike Phenomenon in Greece in 2012"], GSEE Labor Institute. www.inegsee.gr/wp-content/uploads/2015/07/TETRADIA-TEYXOS-38_FINAL.pdf.

Kentikelenis, A. E., Stubbs, T. H., and King, L. P. (2016) "IMF Conditionality and Development Policy Space, 1985–2014," *Review of International Political Economy*, 23(4), pp. 543–582.

Keynes, J. M. (1936) *The General Theory of Employment, Interest and Money*. London: Macmillan.

Korpi, W. (2006) "Power Resources and Employer-Centered Approaches in Explanations of Welfare States and Varieties of Capitalism: Protagonists, Consenters, and Antagonists," *World Politics*, 58(2), pp. 167–206.

Koukiadaki, A. and Kretsos, L. (2012) "Opening Pandora's Box: The Sovereign Debt Crisis and Labour Market Regulation in Greece," *Industrial Law Journal*, 41(3), pp. 276–304.

Kriesi, H. (2012) "The Political Consequences of the Financial and Economic Crisis in Europe: Electoral Punishment and Popular Protest," *Swiss Political Science Review*, 18(4), pp. 518–522.

Lang, V. (2021) "The Economics of the Democratic Deficit: The effect of IMF Programs on Inequality," *Review of International Organizations*, 16(3), pp. 599–623.

Lee, S. K. (2021) "The Politics of Anti-Austerity Protest: South Korea in 1997–1998 and Greece in 2009–2010," *International Journal of Comparative Sociology*, 62(1), pp. 32–55.

Lopes, J. D. S. (2003) "The Role of the State in the Labour Market: Its Impact on Employment and Wages in Portugal as Compared with Spain," *South European Society and Politics*, 8(1–2), pp. 269–286.

Mabbett, D. and Schelkle, W. (2015) "What Difference Does Euro Membership Make to Stabilization? The Political Economy of International Monetary Systems Revisited," *Review of International Political Economy*, 22(3), pp. 508–534.

Magone, J. M. (2014) "Portugal Is Not Greece: Policy Responses to the Sovereign Debt Crisis and the Consequences for the Portuguese Political Economy," *Perspectives on European Politics and Society*, 15(3), pp. 346–360.

Maltezou, R. and Melander, I. (2011) "Clashes in Greece As EU and IMF Start Key Visit," May 12. www.reuters.com/article/us-greece-eu-imf-idUSTRE7497DX20110512.

Mazower, M. (2011) "Democracy's Cradle, Rocking the World," *New York Times*, June 29. www.nytimes.com/2011/06/30/opinion/30mazower.html.

Metinsoy, S. (2022) "'Selective Friendship at the Fund': United States Allies, Labor Conditions, and the International Monetary Fund's Legitimacy," *Politics and Governance*, 10(3), pp. 143–154.

Möller, J. (2015) "Did the German Model Survive the Labor Market Reforms?," *Journal for Labour Market Research*, 48(2), pp. 151–168.

Moury, C. and Standring, A. (2017) "'Going Beyond the Troika': Power and Discourse in Portuguese Austerity Politics," *European Journal of Political Research*, 56(3), pp. 660–679.

Murphy, R. and Farrell, D. M. (2002) "Party Politics in Ireland," in Webb, P., Farrell, D., and Holliday, I. (eds.) *Political Parties in Advanced Industrial Democracies*, Oxford: Oxford University Press, pp. 217–247.

Nelson, S. C. (2014) "Playing Favorites: How Shared Beliefs Shape the IMF's Lending Decisions," *International Organization*, 68(2), pp. 297–328.

Nelson, S. C. (2017) *The Currency of Confidence*. Ithaca, NY: Cornell University Press.

Nelson, S. C. and Wallace, G. P. R. (2017) "Are IMF Lending Programs Good or Bad for Democracy?," *Review of International Organizations*, 12(4), pp. 523–558.

New York Times (2012) "Thousands Protest Austerity Measures in Spain and Portugal," September 15. www.nytimes.com/2012/09/16/world/europe/large-anti-austerity-protests-in-spain-portugal.html.

Nooruddin, I. and Rudra, N. (2014) "Are Developing Countries Really Defying the Embedded Liberalism Compact?," *World Politics*, 66(4), pp. 603–640.

Nooruddin, I. and Simmons, J. W. (2006) "The Politics of Hard Choices: IMF Programs and Government Spending," *International Organization*, 60(4), pp. 1001–1033.

Ó Riain, S. (2014) *The Rise and Fall of Ireland's Celtic Tiger: Liberalism, Boom and Bust*. Cambridge: Cambridge University Press.

O'Hora, A. (2013) "Nobel Economist Stiglitz: 'I'm Astonished at Irish Ability to Suck Up Austerity Pain'," *Irish Independent*, November 8. https://bit.ly/47YeQxE.

Oberdabernig, D. A. (2013) "Revisiting the Effects of IMF Programs on Poverty and Inequality," *World Development*, 46, pp. 113–142.

OECD (2017) "Economic Surveys: Latvia." https://web-archive.oecd.org/2017-10-30/449742-Latvia-2017-OECD-economic-survey-overview.pdf.

Papapetrou, E. (2006) "The Unequal Distribution of the Public–Private Sector Wage Gap In Greece: Evidence from Quantile Regression," *Applied Economics Letters*, 13(4), pp. 205–210.

Pappas, T. S. and O'Malley, E. (2014) "Civil Compliance and 'Political Luddism': Explaining Variance in Social Unrest during Crisis in Ireland and Greece," *American Behavioral Scientist*, 58(12), pp. 1592–1613.

Pastor, M. (1987) "The Effects of IMF Programs in the Third World: Debate and Evidence from Latin America," *World Development*, 15(2), pp. 249–262.

Patra, E. (2012) *Social Dialogue and Collective Bargaining in Times of Crisis: The Case of Greece*. Geneva: ILO.

Pion-Berlin, D. (1983) "Political Repression and Economic Doctrines: The Case of Argentina," *Comparative Political Studies*, 16(1), pp. 37–66.

Piore, M. J. (1983) "Labor Market Segmentation: To What Paradigm Does It Belong?," *American Economic Review*, 73(2), pp. 249–253

Prosser, T. (2016) "Dualization or Liberalization? Investigating Precarious Work in Eight European countries," *Work, Employment and Society*, 30(6), pp. 949–965.

Przeworski, A. and Vreeland, J. R. (2000) "The Effect of IMF Programs on Economic Growth," *Journal of Development Economics*, 62(2), pp. 385–421.

Psimitis, M. (2011) "The Protest Cycle of Spring 2010 in Greece," *Social Movement Studies*, 10(2), pp. 191–197.

Regan, A. (2012) "The Political Economy of Social Pacts in the EMU: Irish Liberal Market Corporatism in Crisis," *New Political Economy*, 17(4), pp. 465–491.

Reinsberg, B., Kern, A., Heinzel, M., and Metinsoy, S. (2023) "Women's Leadership and the Gendered Consequences of Austerity in the Public Sector: Evidence from IMF programs," *Governance* (online first). https://doi.org.10.1111/gove.12764.

Reinsberg, B., Stubbs, T., Kentikelenis, A., and King, L. (2019) "The Political Economy of Labor Market Deregulation during IMF Interventions," *International Interactions*, 45(3), pp. 532–559.

Reinsberg, B., Stubbs, T., and Bujnoch, L. (2022) "Structural Adjustment, Alienation, and Mass Protest," *Social Science Research*, 109, pp. 1–15.

Reuters (2009) "Tens of Thousands of Irish workers Protest in Streets," November 6. www.reuters.com/article/ireland-protest-idUSL667311020091106

Reuters (2013) "Portuguese Stage General Strike against Relentless Austerity," June 27. www.reuters.com/article/us-portugal-strike-transport-idUSBRE95Q09N20130627.

Rickard, S. J. and Caraway, T. L. (2014) "International Negotiations in the Shadow of National Elections," *International Organization*, 68(3), 701–720.

Rickard, S. J. and Caraway, T. L. (2019) "International Demands for Austerity: Examining the Impact of the IMF on the public sector," *Review of International Organizations*, 14(1), pp. 35–57.

Robertson, G. B. and Teitelbaum, E. (2011) "Foreign Direct Investment, Regime Type, and Labor Protest in Developing Countries," *American Journal of Political Science*, 55, 665–677. https://doi-org.eur.idm.oclc.org/10.1111/j.1540-5907.2011.00510.x.

Rodrik, D. (1998) "Why Do More Open Economies Have Bigger Governments?," *Journal of Political Economy*, 106(5), pp. 997–1032.

Rogowski, R. (1989) *Commerce and Coalitions*. Princeton, NJ: Princeton University Press.

Rueda, D. (2012) "Dualization and Crisis," *Swiss Political Science Review*, 18(4), pp. 523–530.

Rueda, D. (2014) "Dualization, Crisis and the Welfare State," *Socio-Economic Review*, 12(2), pp. 381–407.

Shorter, E. and Tilly, C. (1974) *Strikes in France 1830–1968*. Cambridge: Cambridge University Press.

Sidell, S. R. (1988) *The IMF and Third-World Political Instability : Is There a Connection?* New York: St. Martin's Press.

Silva, C. T. (2022) "Protests in Europe in Times of Crisis: The Case of Greece, Ireland and Portugal," *European Journal of Social Sciences*, 5(2), pp. 97–109.

Steinwand, M. C. and Stone, R. W. (2008) "The International Monetary Fund: A Review of the Recent Evidence," *Review of International Organizations*, 3(2), pp. 123–149.

Stone, R. W. (2008) "The Scope of IMF Conditionality," *International Organization*, 62(4), pp. 589–620.

Stroup, C. and Zissimos, B. (2013) "Social Unrest in the Wake of IMF Structural Adjustment Programs," CESifo Working Paper No. 4211.

Stubbs, T., Reinsberg, B., Kentikelenis, A., and King, L. (2020) "How to Evaluate the Effects of IMF Conditionality: An Extension of Quantitative Approaches and an Empirical Application to Public Education Spending," *Review of International Organizations*, 15, pp. 29–73.

Thelen, K. (2012) "Varieties of Capitalism: Trajectories of Liberalization and the New Politics of Social Solidarity," *Annual Review of Political Science*, 15(1), pp. 137–159.

Thelen, K. (2014) *Varieties of Liberalization and the New Politics of Social Solidarity*. Cambridge: Cambridge University Press.

Tilly, C. (1978) *From Mobilization to Revolution*. Reading, MA: Addison–Wesley.

Tilly, C. (2003) *The Politics of Collective Violence*. Cambridge: Cambridge University Press (Cambridge Studies in Contentious Politics).

Trantidis, A. (2014) "Reforms and Collective Action in a Clientelist System: Greece during the Mitsotakis Administration (1990–93)," *South European Society and Politics*, 19(2), pp. 215–234.

Vreeland, J. R. (2002) "The Effect of IMF Programs on Labor," *World Development*, 30(1), pp. 121–139.

Vreeland, J. R. (2003) *The IMF and Economic Development*. Cambridge: Cambridge University Press.

Vreeland, J. R. (2007) *The International Monetary Fund: Politics of Conditional Lending*. New York: Routledge.

Walter, S. (2013) *Financial Crises and the Politics of Macroeconomic Adjustments*. Cambridge: Cambridge University Press.

Walter, S. (2016) "Crisis Politics in Europe: Why Austerity Is Easier to Implement in Some Countries Than in Others," *Comparative Political Studies*, 49(7), pp. 841–873.

Walton, J. and Ragin, C. (1990) "Global and National Sources of Political Protest: Third World Responses to the Debt Crisis," *American Sociological Review*, 55(6), pp. 876–890.

Western, B. (2020) *Between Class and Market*. Princeton, NJ: Princeton University Press.

Woods, N. (2006) *The Globalizers*. Ithaca, NY: Cornell University Press.

Wyszynski, K. and Marra, G. (2018) "Sample Selection Models for Count Data in R," *Computational Statistics*, 33, pp. 1385–1412.

Yusuf, S. and Nabeshima, K. (2012) *Some Small Countries Do It Better: Rapid Growth and Its Causes in Singapore, Finland, and Ireland*. Washington, DC: World Bank. https://openknowledge.worldbank.org/server/api/core/bitstreams/178c4a7b-616f-5820-ab5e-76275a1cc538/content.

Zimmermann, K .F. (2005) "European Labour Mobility: Challenges and Potentials," *De Economist*, 153(4), pp. 425–450.

Acknowledgments

My special thanks to David Doyle for his guidance, support, and encouragement throughout the process of conducting this research. I also would like to thank Merih Angin, Ben Ansell, Nancy Bermeo, Lawrence Broz, Simone Dietrich, Axel Dreher, Ferdinand Eibl, Niamh Hardiman, Stephanie Rickard, Eyal Rubinson, Jaemin Shim, Lawrence Whitehead, and participants at the Oxford University SEESOX colloquium, the University of Groningen IPE colloquium, and the 10th Annual Conference of The Political Economy of International Organizations (PEIO) in Salzburg (January 2019) for their extremely helpful comments and suggestions. I am also indebted to Susan Staggenborg and David Meyer and two anonymous reviewers for their constructive feedback and comments. And many thanks also to Eline Koopman and Maria Sativa Baumann for their excellent research assistance and to Hobie Kropp for meticulously proofreading the manuscript.

Cambridge Elements

Contentious Politics

About the series

Cambridge Elements series in Contentious Politics provides an important opportunity to bridge research and communication about the politics of protest across disciplines and between the academy and a broader public. Our focus is on political engagement, disruption, and collective action that extends beyond the boundaries of conventional institutional politics. Social movements, revolutionary campaigns, organized reform efforts, and more or less spontaneous uprisings are the important and interesting developments that animate contemporary politics; we welcome studies and analyses that promote better understanding and dialogue.

Cambridge Elements

Contentious Politics

Elements in the series

The Phantom at The Opera: Social Movements and Institutional Politics
Sidney Tarrow

The Street and the Ballot Box: Interactions Between Social Movements and Electoral Politics in Authoritarian Contexts
Lynette H. Ong

Contested Legitimacy in Ferguson: Nine Hours on Canfield Drive
Joshua Bloom

Contentious Politics in Emergency Critical Junctures: Progressive Social Movements during the Pandemic
Donatella della Porta

Collective Resistance to Neoliberalism
Paul Almeida and Amalia Pérez Martín

Mobilizing for Abortion Rights in Latin America
Mariela Daby and Mason W. Moseley

Black Networks Matter: The Role of Interracial Contact and Social Media in the 2020 Black Lives Matter Protests
Matthew David Simonson, Ray Block Jr, James N. Druckman, Katherine Ognyanova, and David M. J. Lazer

Law, Mobilization, and Social Movements How Many Masters?
Whitney K. Taylor, Sidney Tarrow

Have Repertoire, Will Travel: Nonviolence as Global Contentious Performance
Selina R. Gallo-Cruz

Aggrieved Labor Strikes Back: Inter-sectoral Labor Mobility, Conditionality, and Unrest under IMF Programs
Saliha Metinsoy

A full series listing is available at: www.cambridge.org/ECTP

www.ingramcontent.com/pod-product-compliance
Ingram Content Group UK Ltd.
Pitfield, Milton Keynes, MK11 3LW, UK
UKHW022146080726
473066UK00010B/799

* 9 7 8 1 0 0 9 4 5 5 7 8 7 *